FIRST ENCOUNTERS

NEW ZEALAND 1642-1840

Edited by Gordon Ell and Sarah Ell

Oratia

PHOTOGRAPH CREDITS: Cover: Lauvergne, Barthelemy, 1805–71, Plage de Korora-reka (Nouvelle Zelande)/Lauvergne del; Hemely sc.; de Sainson edit; Finot imp – [Paris; A. Betrand, 1835], B-098-005, Alexander Turnbull Library; see full image on page 5. Back cover from top: see following pages for information: 7, 86, 29, 46; third image iStock (quill: artisteer, 629999022; journal: Jarin13, 462251535). Title page: see p. 48; p. 7: Établissement des missionnaires anglais a Kidikidi, (Nouvelle-Zélande.) (English missionary settlement at Kerikeri, New Zealand), 1826, by Antoine Chazal, Louis François Lejeune, Ambroise Tardieu. Gift of Horace Fildes, 1937. Te Papa (1992-0035-1815); p. 14: Pixabay; p. 29: Kororareka Beach, Bay of Islands, New Zealand, circa 1856, by Thomas Gardiner. Purchased 1993 with New Zealand Lottery Grants Board funds. Te Papa (1993-0029-1); p. 46: Rex Nan Kivell Collection, NK628/11, National Library or Australia; p. 64: A wounded Hongi Hika and his family, painted by Augustus Earle, PUBL-0115-02, Alexander Turnbull Library; p. 84: Cook Strait, New Zealand, c. 1884, London, by Nicholas Chevalier. Purchased 2003. Te Papa (2003-0034-1).

Published by Oratia Books, Oratia Media Ltd, 783 West Coast Road, Oratia, Auckland 0604, New Zealand (www.oratia.co.nz)

The text is selected and abridged from *Adventurous Times in Old New Zealand: First-hand accounts of the lawless days*, published by Bush Press Communications Ltd, 1994; also republished as *Explorers, Whalers and Tattooed Sailors*, published by Random House, 2008.

ISBN 978-0-947506-90-2

Managing editor: Carolyn Lagahetau
Designer: Sarah Elworthy

The publisher acknowledges the generous support of Creative New Zealand for this publication.

Contestable Fund Grant recipient 2017

ARTS COUNCIL OF NEW ZEALAND TOI AOTEAROA

Let's do the right thing

First published 2021
Printed in China

CONTENTS

INTRODUCTION

The stories in this book have been gathered from personal accounts by the first Europeans to visit or settle in New Zealand. They illustrate the various reasons Europeans came here in the years before the Treaty of Waitangi was signed, and the response from Māori, the tangata whenua (people of the land).

Initial encounters between the first Europeans to visit the distant islands of New Zealand, from Abel Tasman in 1642, were not promising. The capacity for misunderstanding between European cultures and that of Māori tribes extended far beyond the lack of common language. Their basic beliefs and values belonged to completely different worlds. Māori may have appeared as 'savages' to the first Europeans on these shores, but in fact their complex codes of honour justified every aspect of their response to the invaders. Looking back, with the hindsight of our bicultural heritage, it may appear surprising that there were not more conflicts. The tellers of these tales often show glimpses of an understanding of Māori culture which may well have saved their lives.

As the years passed, knowledge of each other's language and customs grew, and Europeans settled tentatively along the shores of Aotearoa. The accounts of sealers and whalers stand alongside those of missionaries and traders, as well as the occasional artist and scientist exploring the frontiers of the world they knew.

The exploration of early New Zealand was the product of an expansionist phase of the European world. The people who came here were themselves of differing cultures — British, French and North American in particular. They brought with them their own cultures, and the motives of each individual varied in intent. The Europeans of the early nineteenth century also had their own political rivalries and traditional enmities. In this book it is easy to sense the personal judgements made by each author. Far from being all of a kind, the adventurers who found their way to our shores did so with a variety of motives and mixed success.

Some of the first were concerned with the repair and equipment of ships. The first entrepreneurs were felling the kauri trees of the north for their timbers late in the eighteenth century. Cordage for those ships, too, could be found on the New Zealand coast, in the form of harakeke, misnamed 'hemp' or 'flax' for its structural qualities. In the farther south of the country, vast herds of fur seals occupied the subantarctic rocks. Sealing gangs, usually on behalf of Sydney operators, were dropped in remote fiords or on islets to conduct the slaughter of seals for skins and blubber. Later, whalers operated on- and offshore.

Missionaries, wanting to spread their Christian faith to the Māori people, were other early arrivals. While it is easy today to be critical of their manner, the missionaries were among the first to record the language and customs of Māori, in an effort to comprehend their values. The bravery of those men who stood between the warring tribes of Māori prevented some of the slaughter which followed the introduction of European weapons such as muskets.

Among the adventurers were men of culture and accomplishment. Artists such as Augustus Earle left not only the first visual images

of New Zealand but also their lesser-known diaries, recording their feelings about the places they painted. Scientists like Ernst Dieffenbach and observers like Edward Jerningham Wakefield were also drawn to record this unfamiliar country.

By the late 1830s, European interest in the islands of New Zealand had progressed to the point where both Britain and France had plans for settlement. Around 2000 Europeans had made their homes about the shores of this lawless land when the Treaty of Waitangi was signed, between the British Crown and Māori chiefs, in February 1840. But it is of the days prior to the treaty that these authors write. Their first-hand accounts give a vivid and often surprising picture of those interesting, challenging and adventurous times.

By their very nature, these accounts are Eurocentric. Few written records exist to give a tangata whenua perspective of these early encounters. However, we can learn, from both the descriptions of Māori culture and the authors' perceptions of it, about traditions and practices, and European attitudes towards them.

A NOTE ON THE EDITING

Much of the text of this book has been taken directly from old books, dating back to the early nineteenth century. Consequently, spelling and occasionally meanings vary with the style of the times. A few obvious and misleading errors have been corrected but generally the style of expression has been left in its original form, so the extracts retain their original flavour.

The rendition of Māori words, from what was then purely an oral language, varies widely between authors. Generally, Māori words in the text have been left as their authors recorded them, with notes on possible translations.

Distances and areas are given in their original imperial form, with a mile equal to 1.6 kilometres and an acre being 0.4 of a hectare. At sea, a nautical mile is still a nautical mile, of some 1.852 kilometres, and a fathom, used to measure the depth of water, is equal to 1.8 metres.

FIRST CONTACTS

MURDERERS' BAY

ABEL TASMAN, 1642

Abel Tasman (?1603–1659) was the leader of the first-known European expedition to encounter Aotearoa, in 1642. The discovery, made in the course of a 33,000 kilometre search for the fabled Great South Land, led him to believe he had encountered the western edge of a great continent stretching to South America. However, neither Tasman nor any of the men from his ships Heemskerck *and* Zeehaen *set foot on the land.*

The Dutch crew first came upon the wild coasts of Westland, then encountered the Ngāti Tūmatakōkiri people of what is now known as Golden Bay as their ships lay at anchor offshore. Efforts to communicate with Māori, blowing trumpets in response to the challenge of conch shells, may have added to the misunderstanding between two vastly different cultures. Tasman tells of a 'massacre' that followed the next morning, while officers of the two ships were holding a council meeting to plan their landing.

After the misadventure recounted here, the Tasman expedition sailed up the North Island coast, unable to make landfall, and returned to the Dutch East India Company's base in Batavia (Java) via Tonga and Fiji.

18th December 1642 In the morning we weighed anchor in calm weather; at noon latitude estimated 40° 49'; longitude, 191° 41'; course kept east-south-east; sailed 11 miles. In the morning before weighing anchor, we had resolved, with the officers of the *Zeehaen*, that we should try to get ashore here, and find a good harbour;

Abel Tasman and his family, 1637.

Jacob Gerritsz, 1594–1651?, PIC T267 NK3, National Library of Australia

and that, as we neared it, we should send out the pinnace to reconnoitre. … In the afternoon our Skipper Ide Tercxsen and our Pilot-major Francoys Jacobz, in the pinnace, and Supercargo [Isaack] Gilsemans, with one of the second mates of the *Zeehaen*, in the latter's cock-boat, went on before to seek a fitting anchorage and a good watering-place. At sunset when it fell calm, we dropped anchor in 15 fathoms, good anchoring-ground; in the evening, about an hour after sunset, we saw a number of lights on shore, and four boats close inshore, two of which came towards us, upon which our own two boats returned on board; they reported that they found no less than 13 fathoms water, and that

Nautical terms

pinnace, cock-boat small boats, propelled by either sails or oars, carried aboard a larger ship and used for short journeys and trips ashore, or transferring goods

supercargo person representing the ship's owner on board a merchant ship, responsible for the cargo. Abel Tasman's expedition was funded by a trading company, and his ships carried goods for trade.

when the sun sank behind the high land they were still about half a mile from shore. When our men had been on board for the space of about one glass the men in the two prows began to call out to us in a rough, hollow voice, but we could not understand a word of what they said. We, however, called out to them in answer, upon which they repeated their cries several times, but came no nearer than a stone-shot; they also blew several times on an instrument of which the sound was like that of a Moorish trumpet; we then ordered one of our sailors (who had some knowledge of trumpet-blowing) to play them some tunes in answer. Those on board the *Zeehaen* ordered their second mate (who had come out to India as a trumpeter, and had in the

Abel Tasman's ships the *Zeehaen* and the *Heemskerk*, with two Maori men outlined against the skyline. This view, with its large Maori figures compared to the reduced size of Tasman's ships, is thought to have given rise to the European belief that Maori were giants.

Gilsemans, Isaack, 1606?–1646, PUBL-0105-004, Alexander Turnbull Library

Mauritius been appointed second mate by the council of that fortress and the ships) to do the same; after this had been repeated several times on both sides, and, as it was getting more and more dark, those in the Natives prows at last ceased, and paddled off. For more security, and to be on our guard against all accidents, we ordered our men to keep double watches, as we are wont to do when out at sea, and to keep in readiness all necessaries of

glass a unit of time aboard ship, measured by sand running through an hourglass. One glass was equal to half an hour.

watch a period of time a team of sailors would be on duty (usually eight glasses, or four hours) before taking a break.

orlap/orlop one of the lower decks of a sailing ship

war, such as muskets, pikes, and cutlasses. We cleaned the guns on the upper-orlap, and placed them again, in order to prevent surprises, and be able to defend ourselves, if these people should happen to attempt anything against us. …

19th Early in the morning a boat manned with thirteen Natives approached to about a stone's cast from our ships; they called out several times, but we did not understand them, their speech not bearing any resemblance to the vocabulary given us by the Hon. Governor-General and Councillors of India, which is hardly to be wondered at, seeing that it contains the language of the Salomonis [Solomon] Islands, &c. As far as we could observe, these people were of ordinary height; they had rough voices and strong bones, the colour of their skin being between brown and yellow; they wore tufts of black hair right upon the top of their heads, tied fast in the manner of the Japanese at the back of the heads, but somewhat longer and thicker, and surmounted by a large, thick white feather. Their boats consisted of two long narrow prows side by side, over which a number of planks or other seats were placed in such a way that those above can look through the water underneath the vessel; their paddles are upward of a fathom in length, narrow and pointed at the end; with these vessels they could make considerable speed.

'A view of Murderers' Bay ...' Isaak Gilsemans was with Abel Tasman when he visited New Zealand in 1642. This is his depiction of the tragedy at Murderers' Bay.

Gilsemans, Isaack, 1606?–1646, PUBL-0086-021, Alexander Turnbull Library

For clothing, as it seemed to us, some of them wore mats, others cotton stuffs; almost all of them were naked from the shoulders to the waist. We repeatedly made signs for them to come on board of us, showing them white linen and some knives that formed part of our cargo. They did not come nearer, however, but at last paddled back to shore.

In the meanwhile, at our summons sent the previous evening, the officers of the *Zeehaen* came on board of us, upon which we convened a council, and resolved to go as near the shore as we could, since there was good anchoring-ground here, and these people apparently sought our friendship. Shortly after we had drawn up this resolution we saw seven more boats put off from the shore, one of which (high and pointed in front, manned with seventeen Natives) paddled round behind the *Zeehaen*; while another, with thirteen able-bodied men in her, approached to within half a stone's throw of our ship. The men in these two boats now and then called out to each other. We held up and showed to them, as before, white linens, &c., but they remained where they were. The skipper of the *Zeehaen* now sent out to them his quartermaster with her cock-boat with six paddlers in it, with orders for the second mates that if these people should offer to come alongside the *Zeehaen* they should not allow too many of them on board of her, but use great caution, and be well on their guard. While the cock-boat of the *Zeehaen* was paddling on its way to her those in the prow nearest to us called out to those who were lying behind the *Zeehaen*, and waved their paddles to them, but we could not make out what they meant. Just as the cock-boat of the *Zeehaen* had put off from board again, those in the prow before us, between the two ships, began to paddle so furiously towards it, that, when they were about half-way, slightly nearer to our ship, they struck the *Zeehaen*'s cock-boat so violently alongside with the stem of their prow that it got a violent lurch, upon which the foremost man in this prow of villains, with a long blunt pike, thrust the quartermaster, Cornelis Jopen, in the neck several times with so much force that the poor man fell overboard. Upon this the other Natives, with short thick clubs, which we at first mistook for heavy blunt parangs, and with their paddles, fell upon the men in the cock-boat, and overcame them by main force, in which fray three of our men were killed and a fourth got mortally wounded through the heavy blows. The quartermaster and two sailors swam to our ship, whence we sent our pinnace to pick them up, which they got into alive. After this outrageous and detestable crime the murderers sent the cock-boat adrift, having taken one of the dead bodies into their prow and thrown another into the sea. Ourselves and those aboard the *Zeehaen*, seeing this, diligently fired our muskets and guns, and though we did not hit any of them, the two

pike long spear or thrusting weapon

parang Malaysian/Indonesian word for a large, heavy knife used as a tool or weapon

weigh anchor lift the anchor and prepare to start sailing

tingang small type of Indonesian boat with a triangular sail

prows made haste to the shore, where they were out of reach of shot. With our fore upper-deck and bow guns we now fired several shots in the direction of their prows, but none of them took effect. Thereupon our Skipper Ide Tercxsen Holman, in command of our pinnace, well manned and armed, rowed towards the cock-boat of the *Zeehaen* (which, fortunately for us, these accursed villains had let drift), and forthwith returned with it to our ships, having found in it one of the men killed and one mortally wounded. We now weighed anchor and set sail, since we could not hope to enter into any friendly relations with these people, or be able to get water or refreshments here. Having weighed anchor and being under sail, we saw twenty-two prows near the shore, of which eleven, swarming with people, were making for our ships. We kept quiet until some of the foremost were within reach of our guns, and then fired one or two shots from the gun-room with our pieces, without, however, doing them any harm; those on board the *Zeehaen* also fired, and in the largest prow hit a man who held a small white flag in his hand, and who fell down. We also heard the cannister-shot strike the prows inside and outside, but could not make out what other damage it had done. As soon as they had got this volley they paddled back to shore with great speed, two of them hoisting a sort of tingang sail. They remained lying near the shore without visiting us further. ...

In this murderous spot (to which we have accordingly given the name of "Moordenaers Bay") we lay at anchor in 40° 50' S. latitude, 191° 30' longitude. From here we shaped our course east-north-east.

A TRAGIC ENCOUNTER

JOSEPH BANKS

When Lieutenant James Cook set out for the Southern Ocean in 1769, his expedition's ships carried a scientific party led by Joseph Banks (1743–1820). Banks was to make his name as a gentleman scientist, and give his name to many plants and places about the Pacific. His diaries reveal a broad interest in anthropology and culture, besides the botany for which he is best remembered. In later life Banks was to become Britain's pre-eminent scientific scholar as President of the Royal Society. Here, Banks tells of the sad human cost of two cultures meeting, when Cook's crew first went ashore at Tūranganui-a-Kiwa (Gisborne) on the east coast of the North Island.

8 October 1769 This morn the land very near us makes in many white cliffs like chalk; the hills are in general clothd with trees, in the valleys some appear to be very large; the whole of the appearance not so fruitfull as we could wish. Stood in for a large bay in hopes of finding a harbour; before we are well within the heads saw several Canoes standing across the bay, who after a little time returnd to the place they came from not appearing to take the least notice of us. Some houses were also seen which appeard low but neat, near one a good many people were collected who sat down on the beach seemingly observing us, possibly the same as we saw in the canoes as they landed somewhere near that place. On a small peninsula

Joseph Banks, painted in 1773. With Dr Carl Solander, Banks collected hundreds of botanical specimens during Cook's first visit to New Zealand.

Mr. Banks, 1773, London, by John Smith, Benjamin West. Purchased 2005 with Ellen Eames Collection funds. Te Papa (2005-0027-1)

at the NE head we could plainly see a regular paling, pretty high, inclosing the top of a hill, for what purpose many conjectures were made: most are of opinion or say at least that it must or shall be either [a] park of Deer or a field of oxen and sheep. By 4 oclock came to an anchor near 2 miles from the shore. The bay appears to be quite open without the least shelter: the two sides of it make in high white Cliffs, the middle is low land with hills gradualy rising behind one another to the chain of high mountains inland. Here we saw many great smoaks, some near the beach others between the hills, some very far within land, which we lookd upon as great indications of a populous country.

In the evening went ashore with the marines &c. March from the boats in hopes of finding water &c. Saw a few of the natives who ran away immediately on seeing us; while we were absent 4 of them attackd our small boat in which there were only 4 boys, they got off from the shore in a river, the people followd them and threatend them with long lances; the pinnace soon came to their assistance, fird upon them and killd the chief. The other three draggd the body about 100 yards and left it. At the report of the musquets we drew together and went to the place where the body was left; he was shot through the heart. He was a middle sized man tattowd in the face on one cheek only in spiral lines very regularly formd; he was coverd with a fine cloth of a manufacture totaly new to us ... ; his hair was also tied in a knot on the top of his head but no feather stuck in it; his complexion brown but not very dark.

Soon after we came on board we heard the people ashore very distinctly talking very loud no doubt, as they were not less than two miles distant from us, consulting probably what is to be done tomorrow.

9. We could see with our glasses but few people on the beach; they walkd with a quick pace towards the river where we landed yesterday, most of these without arms [weapons], 3 or 4 with long Pikes in their hands. The captain orderd three boats to be mannd with seamen and marines intending to land and try to establish a communication with them. A high surf ran on the shore. The Indians [Māori] about 50 remain on the farther side of the river; we lookd upon that as a sign of fear, so landing with the little boat only the Captain, Dr [Carl] Solander, Tupia [Tupaia] and myself went to the river side to speak to them. As soon almost as we appeard they rose up and every man producd either a long pike or a small weapon of well polishd stone about a foot long and thick enough to weigh 4 or 5 pounds, with these they threatned us and signd to us to depart. A musquet was then fird wide of them the ball [small round pieces of metal fired from a musket] of which struck the water, they saw the effect and immediately ceasd their threats. We though[t] that it was prudent to retreat till the marines were landed and drawn up to intimidate them and support us in case of necessity.

They landed and marchd with a [Union] Jack carried before them to a

Captain James Cook.

Rex Nan Kivell Collection, NK1626, National Library of Australia

Tupaia

Tupaia was a Tahitian priest and navigator who accompanied Cook on his expedition to New Zealand. He was recognised by Māori as coming from their ancestral home, and the language he spoke was similar enough to te reo for them to communicate. Many Māori believed Tupaia was in fact in charge of the expedition, and he was treated as an honoured guest.

little bank about 50 yards from the river, which might be about 40 broad; here they were drawn up in order and we again advancd to the river side with Tupia, who now found that the language of the people was so like his own that he could tolerably well understand them and they him. He immediately began to tell them that we wanted provisions and water for which we would give them Iron in exchange: they agreed to the proposal but would by no means lay by their arms which he desird them do: this he lookd upon as a sign of treachery and continualy told us to be upon our guard for they were not our friends. Many words passd the chief purport of which was that each side desired the other to come over to them; at last however an Indian stripd himself and swam over without arms, he was followd by two more and soon

Tūranganui-a-Kiwa

The people that Banks, Cook and the *Endeavour* crew encountered at Tūranganui-a-Kiwa were from four tribes: Te Aitanga-a-Māhaki, Rongowhakaata, Ngāi Tāmanuhiri and Te Aitanga-a-Hauiti. The Tūranganui River, where these first encounters took place, was an important tribal boundary.

The first Māori who encountered Cook's party onshore on 8 October were of Ngāti Oneone (a sub-tribe of Te Aitanga-ā-Hauiti). The first warrior shot and killed was Te Maro of Ngāti Oneone, and the second, the following day, was Te Rakau, an important chief of Rongowhakaata, who had arrived with a party of warriors.

Finnish artist Herman Spöring accompanied Cook on his first voyage to New Zealand. This sketch is his impression of Tolaga Bay.

Sporing, Herman Diedrich, CO18-7474, British Library

The only known drawing made by Tupaia of his time in New Zealand. Tupaia was able to act as an intermediary between Māori and Cook's party because his Tahitian language could be understood by tangata whenua.

MS 15508, f.12, Tupaia, British Library

after by most of the rest who brought with them their arms. We gave them Iron and beads, they seemd to set little value upon either but especialy upon the iron the use of which they certainly were totaly ignorant of. They caught at whatever was offerd them but would part with nothing but a few feathers: their arms indeed they offerd to exchange for ours which they made several atempts to snatch from us; we were upon our guard so much that their attempts faild and they were made to understand that we must kill them if they snatchd any thing from us. After some time Mr Green in turning himself about exposd his hanger [short sword], one of them immediately snatchd it, set up a cry of exultation and waving it round his head retreated gently. It now appeard nescessary for our safeties that so daring an act should be instantly punishd, this I pronouncd aloud as my opinion, the Captain and the rest Joind me on which I fird my musquet which was loaded with small shot, leveling it between his shoulders who was not 15 yards from me.

On the shot striking him he ceasd his cry but instead of quitting his prize continued to wave it over his head retreating as gently as before; the surgeon who was nearer him, seeing this fird a ball at him at which he dropd. Two more who were near him returnd instantly, one seizd his weapon of Green talc [greenstone, pounamu], the other attempted to recover the hanger which the surgeon had scarce time to prevent. The main body of them were now upon a rock a little way in the river. They took [to] the water returning towards us, on which the other three, for we were only 5 in number, fird on them. They then retird and swam again across the river. On their landing we saw that three were wounded, one seemingly a good deal hurt: we may hope however that neither of them were killd as one of the musquets only was loaded with ball, which I think I saw strike the water without taking effect, and Tupias gun which was the last that was fird I clearly saw strike two men low down upon their legs, who probably would be so lame as to walk with difficulty when they landed.

The Indians retird gently carrying with them their wounded and we reembarkd in our boats intending to row round the bay, [and] see if there might be any shelter for a ship on the other side ... We had almost arrivd at the farthest part of the bay when a fresh breze came in from the seaward and we saw a Canoe sailing in standing right towards [us], soon after another paddling. The Captain now resolvd to take one of these which in all probability might be done without the least resistance as we had three boats full of men and the canoes seemd to be fishermen, who probably were without arms. The boats were drawn up in such a manner that they could not well escape us: the padling canoe first saw us and made immediately for the nearest land, the other saild on till she was in the midst of us before she saw us, as soon as she did she struck her sail and began to paddle so briskly that she outran our boat; on a musquet being fird over her she however immediately ceasd padling and the people in her, 7 in all, made all possible haste to strip as we thought to leap into the water, but no sooner did our boat come up with her than they began with stones, paddles &c, to make so brisk a resistance that we were obligd to fire into her by which 4 were killd. The other three who were boys leapd overboard, one of them swam with great agility and when taken made every effort in his power to prevent being taken into the boat, the other two were more easily prevaild upon. As soon as they were in they squatted down expecting no doubt instant death, but on finding themselves well usd [used/treated] and that Cloaths were given them they

'A fortified town or village called a hippah (pa), built on a rock at Tolaga in New Zealand'.

Sporing, Herman Diedrich, 1733–71, B-098-012, Alexander Turnbull Library

recoverd their spirits in a very short time and before we got to the ship appeard almost totaly insensible of the loss of their fellows. As soon as they came onboard we offerd them bread to eat of which they almost devourd a large quantity, in the mean time they had Cloaths given them; this good usage had such an effect that they seemd to have intirely forgot every thing that had happned, put on chearfull and lively countenances and askd and answerd questions with a great deal of curiosity. Our dinner came, they expressd a curiosity to taste whatever they saw us eat, and did; salt pork seemed to please them better than any thing else, of this they eat a good deal. At sunset they eat again an enormous quantity of Bread and drank above a quart of water each; we then made them beds upon the lockers and they laid down to sleep with all seeming content imaginable. After dark loud voices were heard ashore as last night. Thus ended the most disagreeable day My life has yet seen, black be the mark for it and heaven send that such may never return to embitter future reflection.

MOEHANGA – THE FIRST MĀORI TO VISIT ENGLAND

JOHN SAVAGE

John Savage's Some Account of New Zealand, *published in 1807, was the first book written entirely about New Zealand. Savage (1770–1838) was born in south London, England, and qualified as a medical doctor. He was appointed assistant surgeon in New South Wales, Australia, in 1802 and a magistrate in 1804, doing duty at the infamous penal colonies of Van Diemen's Land (Tasmania) and Norfolk Island. In June 1805 he was court-martialled for refusing to attend to a settler's wife, and sailed for England.*

The ship stopped at the Bay of Islands, where Savage made observations for his book. From several Māori who wished to go to England with him, he chose a young Ngāpuhi called Moehanga (described here as Moyhanger) to make the journey, becoming the first Māori to visit Europe.

A day or two previously to our departure I had him [Moehanga] equipped in European clothing; it was coarse, and such as is usually worn by sailors at sea; but however it pleased him and all his kindred: he appeared to assume a sort of superiority over his matted acquaintance, and they eyed him in a manner expressive of their idea of his being highly favoured by the fickle goddess. Moyhanger bore up against the last farewell with much resolution; but as our distance from the land increased, his feelings suffered exceedingly. The sun set beautifully over his native island, and his eye dwelt steadfastly upon it till darkness concealed it from further view. The recollection of scenes of youthful happiness, which he was leaving to traverse an element that affords but little of pleasure or repose, frequently brought the big tear into his eye; but Moyhanger was determined to be a man: he sung his evening song and retired to rest.

For several days following Moyhanger looked anxiously to the westward, the direction in which his native land had disappeared, but he soon recovered his spirits, and was not only merry himself but the cause of mirth in others.

Savage's portait of Ngāti Manu chief 'Tiarrah' (Tara or Te Ara) gained him popularity among local Māori, and led to Moehanga offering to sail to Europe with him.

Savage, John, 1770–1838, A-042-018, Alexander Turnbull Library

During the long and dreary course between New Zealand and Cape Horn, Moyhanger preserved a great degree of cheerfulness — his morning and evening song were never forgotten: he amused himself among the sailors, and frequently exercised his talent for mimicry at their expense. ...

We proceeded on our passage to England, and nothing material occurred to excite the attention of Moyhanger: it was however worthy of remark how much his sight and hearing were superior to other persons on board the ship: the sound of a distant gun was distinctly heard, or a strange sail readily discernible by Moyhanger, when no other man on board could hear or perceive them.

At length the long wished for land, the land of promise to Moyhanger, appeared in view, and the abundant supply of fish, meat, and vegetables of an Irish port made a favourable impression upon him respecting our country. The number of ships, from which he estimated our wealth and population, was a constant source of wonder, which upon sailing up to the port of London became perfect astonishment.

I had dispatches for government, and it was necessary I should proceed to London from Cork, by way of Dublin and Hollyhead. The ship was detained several days by contrary winds, during which time Moyhanger regretted my absence in a most affectionate manner.

Upon the arrival of the ship in the River Thames, I went to meet Moyhanger, who was very much pleased to see me. The great quantity of shipping, and the appearance of London altogether excited a degree of surprise greater than any he had heretofore experienced; but it gave rise to a reflection that cast a gloom upon his countenance. He told me that in New Zealand he was a man of some consequence, but he saw that in such a country as he was now in, his consideration must be entirely lost: however, Moyhanger never took anything to heart for any length of time, and he accompanied me to the shore with great cheerfulness.

This immense metropolis has amazed the most enlightened; it will not therefore appear extraordinary that an uncultivated native of the antipodes should be struck with the greatest possible degree of wonder. We landed at the easternmost part of the town, and had some distance to walk before we could procure a hackney coach: he had during this perambulation something to admire in everything he saw. The shops with immense stores of ironmongery excited much his attention; as we passed houses where these articles were presented for sale, he always observed to me, Piannah Oota nua nua tokee very good country, plenty of iron. Commodities of real utility uniformly claimed his first consideration. The shops that exhibited articles of dress and ornamental finery excited his laughter; while those that displayed substantial cloathing appeared to give him real satisfaction. Through the part of the town we had to walk, there are many shops of the latter description; whenever he passed one, he observed to me, Piannah, nue nue Kakahow — This is very good, there is plenty of cloathing.

The sailors had learnt him the familiar mode of address, How do you do, my boy?

Moyhanger found it very useful in his walk, for the singularity of his appearance attracted much notice from the passengers: they frequently stood to gaze at him. Moyhanger had a vast deal of good nature, and whenever he observed this, he faced about and offered his hand, with, How do you do, my boy? His appearance intimidated many, and they withdrew from his proffered shake by the hand.

The coach gave him great satisfaction: when the horses first started off, the motion seemed to alarm him a little; but with me he soon gained confidence. He looked out on each side — then in front — then appeared thoughtful. I asked him how he liked our present situation: he replied, Piannah wurrie nuenue yaieda — Very good house, it walks very fast.

As we passed through a number of streets in our way to my lodgings, at the west end of the town, nothing escaped his observation. The church steeples — the shops — the passengers the horses and carriages, all called forth some singular remark. Of the height of the steeples he observed, Piannah wurrie tuwittee tuwitte paucoora — very good house, it goes up to the clouds. On noticing any singularities, decrepitude, lameness, or infirmity, in a passenger, he always remarked, Kioòda tungata, or Kioòda wyenna — Good for nothing man or woman. His eye was constantly seeking articles of iron, cloathing or food. Of some of the streets he observed, Nue nue tungata, nue nue wurrie, ittee ittee eka, ittee ittee potatoe — Plenty of men, plenty of

---

Early written Māori

At this time, Māori was solely an oral language, and these are among the first attempts to record it phonetically. Some words can be recognised and translated:

nua probably nui, big

tokee probably toki, axe

kakahow kākahu, clothes

wurrie whare, house

tungata tangata, man/person

wyenna wahine, woman

ittee iti, small

eka ika, fish

noho noho, to sit

racoo rākau, wood

kikie kai, food

When Moehanga uses 'tippeehee' to mean chief, he was probably referring to Te Pahi, the senior chief from his area of the Bay of Islands.

William Wentworth-Fitzwilliam, 4th Earl Fitzwilliam, 1786. Savage writes about the visit Moehanga made to the Earl's home.

Yale Center for British Art, Paul Mellon Collection, B1977.14.9933

houses, but very little fish, and very few potatoes.

I never could make Moyhanger pronounce the word England, therefore I was content to allow him to make use of Europe in its stead, which he pronounced without difficulty. Some times on our way he would draw a comparison between this country and his own, which appeared to give rise to melancholy reflections. He would say, Nue nue Europe, ittee ittee New Zealand.

We arrived at my lodging, where Moyhanger joined my servant boy, who had been his companion during our passage to England, and he appeared perfectly happy.

Soon after my arrival I introduced Moyhanger to Earl Fitzwilliam. I told him that his lordship was a chief, and Moyhanger entered the mansion with becoming respect. The furniture and paintings pleased him highly, but with the affability of his lordship, and the Countess Fitzwilliam, he was quite delighted. ...

He whispered to me whenever Lord Fitzwilliam turned his back, Piannah tippeehee — Very good chief; and with her ladyship and the company he was equally pleased.

The ornamental parts of the furniture did not make such an impression upon him, as might be imagined: Of the mirrors, and other splendid ornaments, he merely observed, Miti — they are very fine; and while I thought he was admiring the more striking objects, I found he was counting the chairs. He had procured a small piece of stick, which he had broken into a number of pieces to assist his recollection. He observed, Nue nue tungata noho tippeehee — A great number of men sit with the chief.

London, 1860.

Yale Center for British Art, Paul
Mellon Collection, B1986.29.217

Moyhanger departed highly delighted with his visit; he frequently requested me to repeat it, and often enquired after the health of the chief and his family.

It was extremely inconvenient to take Moyhanger to public exhibitions, or even to walk with him in the streets, on account of John Bull's [a name for the English people] curiosity: I did therefore not shew him so many of the lions as I otherwise would have done. I accompanied him to St. Paul's cathedral: the vast dimensions of this pile of building appeared to astonish him: the space beneath the dome he contemplated with much satisfaction, but he dwelt with infinite pleasure upon the monuments of our great men.

A great source of entertainment to this native was observing the passengers, making observations upon their faces and persons, and not unfrequently laughing heartily at their expense.

Wooden legs amused him very much. One

MOEHANGA.

FIRST MAORI TO VISIT ENGLAND.

HIS OBSERVATIONS AND INTERESTS.

(By C. R. STRAUBEL).

Most New Zealanders have heard of Hongi and his exploits, but though he is outstanding among the chiefs of his time, he was by no means the first Maori to visit England. At least three of his countrymen had been that far afield a decade before, and many had been to Port Jackson. The three were Moehanga, in 1806; Matara, son of Te Pahi, in 1807; and Ruatara in 1809. The most interesting of these—because he is the first—is Moehanga.

This article about Moehanga's visit was written in 1926, noting his importance as the first Māori to visit England.

Papers Past, Auckland Star, Volume LVII, Issue 288, 4 December 1926

day he saw a man with two; he called me in great haste to observe the unfortunate fellow, saying Tungata cadooa poona poona racoo — Here is a man with two wooden legs.

Noise or scolding he very much disliked; the dissonance of the London cries consequently displeased him; he would, upon these occasions, express himself, Kiooda tungata, or kiooda wyeena nue nue mum mum mum — Bad man or woman to make such a noise.

Our markets afforded him much satisfaction, by enabling him to perceive that we were abundantly supplied with food; indeed the appearance of many of the passengers relieved him of any apprehension of want, if he had previously entertained any such ideas. Whenever he saw a corpulent man pass by he would say, Tungata nue nue kikie — That man has plenty to eat. How such an immense population could be fed was to him, at first, a mystery, seeing no appearance of cattle or cultivation; but the arrival of some droves of oxen, and the waggon loads of vegetables that constantly passed our house, soon relieved him from any apprehension on our account. ...

When he arrives in his own country he will be a very superior man in point of riches and useful knowledge. The use of carpenters' and coopers' tools he is tolerably well acquainted with, and I have no doubt if he remains in New Zealand, that he will remember his visit to Europe with peculiar satisfaction for the remainder of his life.

MISSIONARIES
AND TRADERS

THE FIRST CHRISTMAS

SAMUEL MARSDEN

The Reverend Samuel Marsden (1765–1838) is generally credited with bringing Christianity to New Zealand. As assistant chaplain to the penal colony in New South Wales, he met and hosted Māori chiefs who visited there aboard whaling and early trading ships. On his first visit to New Zealand, aboard the brig Active *in 1814, Marsden celebrated the first Christian service on these shores, under the protection of Ngāpuhi chief Ruatara (called Duaterra here) at Rangihoua in the Bay of Islands. Korokoro of Ngare Raumati and Hongi Hika of Ngāpuhi were also important local chiefs.*

Duaterra passed the remaining part of the day in preparing for the Sabbath. He enclosed about half an acre of land with a fence, erected a pulpit and reading desk in the centre, and covered the whole either with black native cloth or some duck [fabric] which he had brought with him from Port Jackson. He also procured some bottoms of old canoes and fixed them up as seats on each side of the pulpit for the Europeans to sit upon, intending the next day to have Divine service performed there ... He had also erected a flag-staff on the highest hill in the village which had a very commanding view.

On Sunday morning (December 25th) when I was upon deck I saw the English flag flying, which was a pleasing sight in New Zealand. I considered it the signal for the dawn of civilization, liberty, and religion in that dark and benighted land. I never viewed the British colours with more gratification, and flattered myself they would never be removed till the natives of that island enjoyed all the happiness of British subjects.

About ten o'clock we prepared to go ashore to publish the glad tidings of the Gospel for the first time. I was under no apprehensions for the safety of the vessel, and therefore ordered all on board to go on shore to attend Divine service, except the master and one man. When we landed we found Korokoro, Duaterra, and Shunghee [Hongi Hika] dressed in regimentals which [New South Wales] Governor [Lachlan] Macquarie had given them, with their men drawn up ready to march into the enclosure to attend Divine service. They had their swords by their sides and a switch [whip] in their hands. We entered the enclosure and were placed in the seats on each

Samuel Marsden.

Fittler, James, 1758–1835, 23,602,
The Hocken Collections – Te Uare
Taoka o Hakena

The landing of Samuel Marsden at the Bay of Islands, 1814 , as portrayed in the 1920s.

Rex Nan Kivell Collection,
NK4257, National Library
of Australia

side of the pulpit. Korokoro marched his men on and placed them on my right hand in the rear of the Europeans and Duaterra placed his men on the left. The inhabitants of the town with the women and children and a number of other chiefs formed a circle round the whole. A very solemn silence prevailed — the sight was truly impressive. I got up and began the service with singing the Old Hundred Psalm [a well-known hymn], and felt my very soul melt within me when I viewed my congregation and considered the state we were in.

After reading the service, during which the natives stood up and sat down at the signal given by the motion of Korokoro's switch which was regulated by the movements of the Europeans, it being Christmas Day, I preached from the second chapter of St. Luke's Gospel, the tenth verse: 'Behold I bring you glad tidings of great joy.' The natives told Duaterra they could not understand what I meant. He replied they were not to mind that now for they would understand

This image, drawn in the 1890s, depicts Samuel Marsden preaching the first sermon in New Zealand at Oihi Bay, Bay of Islands, in 1814.

7-A1818, Auckland Libraries Heritage Collections

The missionary settlement of Rangihoua, Bay of Islands, painted in the early 1830s.

Rex Nan Kivell Collection, NK131, National Library of Australia

by and by, and that he would explain my meaning as far as he could. When I had done preaching he informed them what I had been talking about. Duaterra was very much pleased that he had been able to make all the necessary preparations for the performance of Divine service in so short a time, and we felt much obliged to him for his attention. He was extremely anxious to convince us that he would do everything for us that lay in his power and that the good of his country was his principal consideration. In the above manner the Gospel has been introduced to New Zealand, and I fervently pray that the Glory of it may never depart from its inhabitants till time shall be no more.

When the service was over we returned on board much gratified with the reception we had met with, and we could not but feel the strongest persuasion that the time was at hand when the Glory of the Lord would be revealed to these poor benighted heathens and that those who were to remain on the island had strong reason to believe that their labours would be crowned and blessed with success.

THE SPAR TRADE

RICHARD A. CRUISE

Richard Alexander Cruise (?1784–1832) was born in Ireland and embarked upon a military career. When he visited New Zealand in 1820 he was a captain in the 84th Regiment of Foot. Detachments from the 69th and 84th regiments had acted as guards on the convict ship HMS Dromedary which, after dropping her cargo of 369 male convicts at 'Hobart's town' and Port Jackson (Sydney), was heading back to England via New Zealand. The crew wanted to obtain suitable tree trunks for use as spars (masts and other rigging for sailing ships), and were accompanied by the Reverend Samuel Marsden and a number of Māori including Ngāpuhi chief Korokoro (called Krokro here). Cruise's Journal of Ten Months' Residence in New Zealand *was published in 1824. Here he writes about attempting to gather timber in the southern Bay of Islands.*

April 8th, Saturday The carpenter and some of the gentlemen went up the river Cowa Cowa [Kawakawa] in the morning, to examine the kaikaterre [kahikatea] that grows on its banks, and to ascertain if it were possible to purchase a cargo of it, in the event of the ship being disappointed in getting cowry [kauri] elsewhere. The current was so rapid from the late rains, that the boat was with great difficulty rowed against it up to the swamp where the timber grew, and the inundation here prevented a near approach to the spars. The Cowa-Cowa is wide and deep for six miles, its banks are generally steep and sometimes perpendicular; and they are richly clothed with trees and shrubs, which grow very thick upon them, and hang over the water in great luxuriance. We saw a number of birds, some of which sang very sweetly; and though the autumn was far advanced, the verdure [greenery/vegetation] of the country was as unimpaired as in the middle of summer.

Where the river begins to get narrow its course is through low and swampy ground; it is often very shallow and very much choked with roots and stumps of trees. At one place we observed a head stuck on a pole, the flesh as yet scarcely decayed. The natives told us it was the head of a slave who had been killed for committing a theft, and that it was exhibited as a warning to others.

In the evening Krokro came on board, and announced the failure of his attempt to get a spar down to Mannawarra [Manawaora] Bay: he said he had cut the tree, dragged it out of the wood, and rolled it down a hill, when it unfortunately stuck in a swamp, and defied all his exertions to get it out.

The purser, who had been absent all day endeavouring to purchase provisions, returned at eight in the evening with some potatoes and five pigs, one of which, the moment it was hoisted in, ran to the opposite gangway and jumped overboard; and though a boat went immediately in pursuit, it could not be found. An hour and a half afterwards the animal came alongside, and was got on board not much the better for its excursion.

Midshipman Perceval Baskerville had the job of keeping the logbook for HMS *Dromedary*.

Baskerville, Perceval, ?–1858, MSY-2983, Alexander Turnbull Library

Kauri logs being
hauled into position
for milling in the
Kaipara, 1839.
Behind the group of
men is a squared-off
log ready to be cut
into planks.

Heaphy, Charles, 1820–1881,
PUBL-011-03, Alexander
Turnbull Library

April 9th, Sunday We had a visit from Tekokee [Te Koki, another Ngāpuhi chief], the proprietor of the timber on the banks of the Cowa-Cowa: he undertook to supply the ship with as many spars as she wanted: at the rate of one spar for each axe, and to float them down the river to her; remarking, that although the swamp was impracticable for Europeans to work in, the New Zealanders [Māori] did not care about it. He was a very strong-built man, quiet and mild in his manners; he was accompanied by a person to whom the whalers had given the name King George [Ngāti Manu chief Te Whareumu]; but this name accorded little with his very moderate pretensions as a chief of the Bay of Islands. . . .

April 10th, Monday Early in the morning the carpenter, boatswain, and some sailors, were sent on shore with purchase-blocks and tackle, to meet Krokro and his people, and assist them in getting the spar out of the mud. Krokro did not make his appearance till one p.m., and instead of 300 men that he promised to bring, he was only attended by seven. After leading the Europeans from one place to another, under pretence of not knowing where the spar was, they at length ascertained that it had never been cut, and that the whole story was a fabrication. . . . In the evening it blew very hard, and there was much difficulty in getting across the bay.

The captain of the *General Gates* came on board the *Dromedary*, and expressed his intention of going soon to sea, having got an ample supply of refreshments in return for powder and muskets.

April 11th, Tuesday The supply of fish from the natives beginning to diminish, the seine [fishing net] was hauled in the evening, but with little success. ...

April 13th We had a visit during the course of the day from our old friend Tetero [Te Toru, chief of the Waikare area]: it was the first he had paid us; and he said he had felt so much ashamed of not having been able to realise the promises he had made during the passage from Port Jackson, of supplying the ship with timber, that he had not been able to prevail upon himself to come near us. . . .

April 16th, Sunday Divine service was performed by Mr. Marsden. One of the soldiers' great-coats having been stolen out of the *Prince Regent* the evening she went to take possession

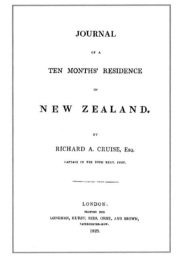

JOURNAL

OF A

TEN MONTHS' RESIDENCE

IN

NEW ZEALAND.

BY

RICHARD A. CRUISE, Esq.

CAPTAIN IN THE 84TH REGT. FOOT.

LONDON:

PRINTED FOR
LONGMAN, HURST, REES, ORME, AND BROWN,
PATERNOSTER-ROW.
1823.

This image of chief Te Toru was on the frontispiece of Cruise's book. Te Toru had travelled with Samuel Marsden to Paramatta, where he had learned English, then returned to the Bay of Islands aboard the *Dromedary* in 1820. He was described as being 45 years old (in 1820) and 6 feet 2 inches (1.88 m) tall.

View of the Kohukohu
River in the Hokianga
in 1839. Kauri spars
are being loaded on
to the ship, while the
rowboat at front is
hauling spars.

Heaphy, Charles, 1820–81, C-025-
014, Alexander Turnbull Library

of the *General Gates*, and a suspicion having fallen upon some of Timoranga's [Te Morenga] tribe, the circumstance was mentioned to this chief, who came on board in the morning. He said he had heard of the theft a few moments before, that he knew who committed it, and that he would recover the property: for which purpose he soon after crossed the bay. . . .

April 18th, Tuesday Early in the morning Timoranga brought back the soldier's coat, and received a present for the trouble he had taken to recover it.

The impossibility of procuring a cargo of cowry in the Bay of Islands was now obvious, and the carpenter had latterly formed a more favourable opinion of the kaikaterra. Of this kind of timber, as has already been observed, there was abundance on the banks of the Cowa-

OPPOSITE: Kororareka,
Bay of Islands,
1841.

Kororareka in the Bay of Islands,
1841, Sydney, by Conrad
Martens. Purchased 2002.
Te Papa (2002-0018-1)

Cowa; and a bargain having been concluded with Tekokee and King George, that they should receive an axe for every spar they brought alongside, the carpenter was despatched to mark the trees, and set the natives to work to fell them. On his reporting that he had completed these arrangements, it was determined to remove the ship as near as possible to the mouth of the Cowa- Cowa, and begin taking in her cargo.

April 19th, Wednesday In the morning, two boats with several men were sent on shore to assist Krokro in cutting down some cowry spars, that he said he had cut. They returned in the afternoon with five, four of which were scarcely large enough to make masts for boats, and the fifth was destined for a top-gallant-yard for the *Dromedary.*

With this last act of deceit our intimacy with Krokro ceased. His influence in this part of the bay was so great, that it must have been an object to him to detain us as long in it as he could. While at anchor in Parro [Pāroa Bay] he considered the ship as his; and it appeared his neighbours had not the power to trade with us without his permission: an indulgence which he seemed almost entirely to withhold from the people of the Wycaddy [Waikare].

The sea-breeze setting in at noon, the ship got under weigh, and moved into Kororadeca [Kororāreka/Russell] Bay.

ENVOY OF PEACE

HENRY WILLIAMS

A naval lieutenant who became an Anglican priest, the Reverend Henry Williams (1782–1867) was a man of action as well as a man of God. He and his family played a leading part in the introduction of Christianity to New Zealand. Sailing his own ship, Williams extended his mission from the Bay of Islands to other regions of the North Island and is credited with drafting the Māori version of the Treaty of Waitangi. He is often described as the 'peacemaker', for sometimes only the moral force of his mission stood between the warring Māori tribes then newly armed with guns. Here he describes acting as a peace-broker between northern tribes, in the wake of the death of the powerful Ngāpuhi chief Hongi Hika.

Thursday, 20 [March, 1828] Between 9 and 10 we took our departure with six native boys in company with Rewa his wife and son. At 11.30 we arrived at his residence at Waimate a beautiful spot in the midst of plantations to a considerable extent. We here took some refreshment expecting to proceed on immediately, but we were detained for 6 hours by Rewa's talking and fitting a lock on a gun. His family formed a very interesting group. About 3 o'clock our party began to move under the guidance of one of Rewa's daughters a girl about 14 carrying a double barrel fowling piece. Rewa had not yet dined. Near sunset we arrived at a settlement of one of Rewa's friends where he overtook us here[;] six large baskets of kumera were immediately turned out for our part. …

Friday, 21 Slept but little as Rewa and a number of women were talking and laughing all night. At the first dawn of day we were in motion and before sunrise on the road. We met persons occasionally who gave us intelligence respecting the movements of the army which quickened our movements as Rewa frequently set off on a run and we were obliged to keep company. We travelled generally thro' level country, and overtook two parties well armed with muskets: they had much curiosity to know our reason for going which Rewa explained. About noon we saw the smoke of the encampment and by 2 arrived at it. We recd. a hearty welcome from our friend and pitched our tents close to Tohitapu. We had a good deal of conversation upon the general disposition of our natives; and some who at Paihia had laughed at the idea of making

Henry Williams.

The life of Henry Williams, Archdeacon of Waimate, 1877, Auckland, by Hugh Carleton, Wilsons & Horton, Printers. Gift of Charles Rooking Carter. Te Papa (RB001168)

In January 1832 Williams and William Fairburn joined a taua (war party) in an effort to prevent Ngāpuhi from attacking Ngāi Te Rangi of Tauranga. Williams and Fairburn are in the vessel at the centre of the image.

PUBL-0031-1835-1, Alexander Turnbull Library

Hone Heke and Patuone.

Hand-coloured lithograph by B. Waterhouse after G.F. Angas, 1846, Rex Nan Kivell Collection, NK55, National Library of Australia

peace, now desired that we should be very bold and determined with the enemy for peace. …

Saturday, 22 Numbers of guns were fired during the night, lest the enemy should surprise the camp. At the first dawn of day all in motion eating their food and preparing for their march and in a few minutes a general rush to the path leading towards the Pa. We with many of the chiefs were about the centre and were hurried along thro' a wood of considerable length and partly through a swamp. There was much rain and thunder, the rain made our walk very uncomfortable and the thunder struck the natives with awe they considered it as a sure indication of a battle. We halted by the side of a hill until all were collected together when two or three chiefs gave an address after which we again moved on and at length came into a beautiful valley opposite the Pa. Kumeras had been planted over the whole plain some portion of which had been taken by Ware Umu's [Te Whareumu] people. The people ran about in every direction some to destroy houses some to fetch food others to see the spot where Ware Umu fell. In the course of 3 hours ranges of booths were formed for the accommodation of the different tribes with the utmost order each tribe sitting by itself. In the afternoon Rewa and Tohitapu consulted with us: they considered that it would not be proper for any of them to go into the Pa today but that we had better go by ourselves and ascertain the real feelings of the natives in the opposite party. We accordingly went to the Pa in company with two natives who had come from thence and relatives of Rewa. We were received very graciously, and conducted to Patuone and many others. They expressed their desire for peace and regret that any fighting had taken place they appeared glad to see us. ... As we passed along to our tent the people drew around to inquire the news and were pleased when we told them that all desired peace. Before sunset I paid a visit round to all the Chiefs, and had some very pleasing conversation with them. It was highly gratifying to observe the order which was preserved amongst such a disordered and independent race. It appeared the general wish for peace should take place on the morrow. ...

Sunday, 23 No bustle in the camp. After breakfast my sheet was hoisted for a flag and Mr. [George] Clarke and I went to the Pa to say that no meeting would take place today as it was the Ratapu [sabbath, Sunday] but before we had concluded breakfast Tohitapu came to ask if the body of Taramauroa a relative of his who had been killed in the late fight should be exposed to public view and to have the pihe [funeral lament] sung over it. ... As soon as night had closed in the natives began to dance and after hakaring [haka] for some time there was a general firing round, many fired ball. Tohitapu who has as little desire for these things as anyone called aloud to twist off the ball [musket balls] before [an] accident happened but notwithstanding all that was said many continued firing ball.

Monday, 24 The eventful day is at last arrived which is to determine the question between these two great powers, the Napui [Ngāpuhi] and the Mahurehure [Te Māhurehure, a Ngāpuhi sub-tribe]. Much rain fell in the night and this morning. Notice was given that Tareha [Tāreha] was at hand. While at breakfast Tohitapu and Rewa came to the tent to consult as to proceedings. Tohitapu did not like the idea of going into the Pa tho' he

Ngāti Hao chief Eruera Maihi Patuone, pictured in later life.

NZG-18920813-802-1, New Zealand Graphic, Auckland Libraries Heritage Collection

had been deputed by the leading men. He however, at length made up his mind to what might await him. Rewa spoke of his desire to go to Waikato to make peace. One of his daughters is married to a Chief belonging there, he thought we had better go up in the vessel. Breakfast being concluded Tohitapu hurried us off to accompany him to the Pa. He requested that the white flag might be planted between the parties which was done on the side of a broad ditch serving as a division between the two armies. The situation was very favourable for the occasion the ground being perfectly level, about three quarters of a mile from the camp and the same from the Pa. After fixing the flag we passed on to the Pa, Tohi's heart beating as he went. We were received in the usual form by Patuone, &c., &c., they sitting on the ground under a shed and the natives pressing upon us on all sides. After a short conversation, the whole of the Natives moved towards the entrance to the Pa, and we with the eldest son of Patuone advanced to the flag which was our station. Several persons of distinction joined in a short time from the Pa. Rewa then came forward from the camp and crossing the ditch rubbed noses with the party from the Pa and took his station with us. Much noise was heard in the camp, and in a short time the various tribes were obs'd [observed] marching in great order with their muskets toward us, winding through some bushes which grew in the road. The sight was very imposing for this part of the world. When about 150 yards off they made a rush accompanied with a horrible yell. There were about 700 men generally armed with muskets. After remaining some time Rewa went forward to the opposite party which was remaining at the bottom of the Pa and saluting the chiefs brought them all forward to within 40 yards of his own people. Several hakas took place on each side and volleys of musketry fired. As it was apprehended that many might fire ball the Chiefs took every possible care to prevent mischief and ordered that the parties should fire to the right and left. When the firing had ceased, Rewa commenced his addressing [in] a manly stile, desiring that peace should be established.

Then followed Patuone and many others. … After the speaking

commenced many from either side withdrew to their respective parties, and a constant firing of guns was kept up towards the camp and Pa, which might be understood as indication of joy, but however it was observed that many shots were fired when the Chiefs abruptly ordered the people to disperse. Messrs. [Richard] Davis and [James] Kemp returned to the camp to order our boys to carry our luggage into the Pa, on our way to the Wesleyan [Methodist] settlement at Mangungu on another branch of the river, while Mr. Clarke and I retired with the Mahurehure into the Pa to look for Mr. [John] Hobbs's boat. On our way many shots passed over our heads, some came very near, and it is a great providence that no one was wounded, for on this precarious foundation humanly speaking depended the fate of the day. When we had entered the Pa the firing ceased and the natives as if released from prison took their canoes and dispersed their respective places of abode.

Henry and his brother William Williams portrayed calming hostile Māori by reading extracts from the Bible in te reo.

PUBL-0151-2-013, Alexander Turnbull Library

SEALERS AND WHALERS

ATTACK BY NIGHT

JOHN BOULTBEE

John Boultbee (1799–1854) was an educated and articulate Englishman who chose to 'rough it' around Australia and the southern part of New Zealand with sealing gangs. After travelling the world, Boultbee arrived in Tasmania in the 1820s, and in 1826 sailed for southern New Zealand on the Elizabeth *with a sealing gang employed by Sydney businessmen Daniel Cooper and Solomon Levey. He spent almost two years working around the coast of Fiordland and Southland, eventually making friends with local Māori despite this early encounter in Fiordland that almost took his life. Boultbee kept a diary of his world travels, which he eventually published as* Journal of a Rambler. *Here he writes about being attacked by local Māori while sealing at Open Bay in South Westland in 1825.*

Our boat was placed ready for launching & lay about 30 yards from the cave in which we slept. Myself & another had been relieved from our 2 hours' watch, about quarter of an hour, & had just dozed a little, when we were startled by the report of a musket, & a confused cry of natives evidently approaching rapidly. We jumped up, & I seized a loaded piece [gun] that lay at my head, & made a hasty retreat out of the cave. Perkins, the Boatsteerer asked 'Where's the muskets' but having no time to reply, I pursued my way: on going out of the cave, I fired the musket towards the natives, who, through the darkness of the night, I could not distinguish individually, they

Cannibalism

Boultbee, like many early European visitors to Aotearoa New Zealand, believed the Māori people were cannibals, and was afraid of being killed and eaten. However, while cannibalism was certainly an occasional practice in Māori society prior to and in the early days of European contact, it was largely a ritual practice associated with warfare.

appearing like a cloud at that time. Whether I hit any body or not I cannot say, & indeed it was no time for conjecture. I ran direct to the boat, where all hands made a simultaneous rush & attempted to launch her, but the close approach of the natives prevented us, & we could not move her. I was on that side of the boat next to the cannibals, as were also 3 others. Seeing we should be cut down if we did not remove our station, we retreated, God knows where. I only recollect I stooped underneath the steer oar which lay over the stern of the boat, & found myself defenseless, petrified with fear & astonishment,

Seal hunting in the 1860s.

Grosse, Frederick, 1828–94, IAN03/03/68/1, State Library, Victoria

standing about 4 yards on the opposite side of the boat: my musket I had laid down in her on endeavouring to launch her, & I had neither balls or powder at hand, & even if I had, I could not get them out of the boat, surrounded as it was by natives, who now kept up a most horrid yell, scarcely human. To describe the state of my mind or feelings at this critical period, would be difficult.

I saw a tall fellow thrusting at me with a spear over the boat's quarter; that instant (& just in time to save my life) I snatched up the after oar (which lay over the stern & which was 15 feet long) & stepping back a pace, swung my oar with all my strength which now exceeded its usual pitch, in this state of desperation, & struck the native on the arm with the blade of my novel weapon. I recollect hearing the spear fall on the pebbly beach, & thought I saw the fellow's arm droop, and it is more than probable, I broke it, as the whole sway of the oar was sufficient to break a stronger thing than a man's arm. Now was the time for life or death. Fear had left me but I cannot say courage supplied its room. I rather imagine it was that kind of desperate feeling that a stag experiences when at bay, where he can no longer flee away from the hounds, & puts his last refuge at stake. When I had got my oar in readiness for another attack, I saw a fellow advancing towards me with a club, screaming most diabolically, & cutting as many capers, as if he had made himself sure of his mark; he also I struck on the temple, & as he instantly fell back with great force on the beach, throwing the pebble stones in my face with his feet as he was falling, I have little doubt that he was not killed. I was now in a continual exertion, striking right &

Muskets

Muskets were a common type of gun. They had a long barrel and fired musket balls — small, round projectiles made of lead — rather than bullets. The guns were difficult to load, especially in the heat of battle. Each musket ball was wrapped in a paper cartridge with a little bit of gunpowder so it could be fired out of the barrel. Each time the gun was fired, a new ball had to be forced down the barrel using a ramrod. Muskets were used by Europen soldiers in the 1700s and 1800s, and were quickly adopted by some Māori tribes, who used them to wreak havoc on their traditionally armed enemies.

John Boultbee made
this portrait of
Ngāi Tahu leader
Te Whakataupuka
about 1827.

qMS-257-02, Alexander
Turnbull Library

left indiscriminately, & without taking aim, but I never failed to come in contact with some one or other with my trusty oar, therefore finding I was able to defend myself, & encouraged by the success of my blows, myself at the same time unhurt, I felt quite void of fear, & with the fury & vengeance of a fiend, I accompanied my blows with strange oaths & invectives against the infernal tribe who were fighting with us. I had also the satisfaction to hear two of my boat mates, firing amongst the natives as often as they could prime & load, & our kangaroo dog, timid as he was, partook of his share of the action, running in amongst, & biting the naked bodies of the natives; who I suspect magnified the size & nature of the dog in the most formidable manner, the darkness of the night preventing them from seeing the smallness of our numbers, & means of defense; & it is providential that it was so, as otherwise they would have most likely have killed every soul of us. …

Having observed that the natives had gone towards the cave, some apparently wounded (evidently groaning), I shouted to my two boat mates & begged them to make haste & try to launch the boat, to which they instantly & joyfully complied, & we had the satisfaction to find ourselves afloat once more & out of danger. Our dog, which at other times used to sneak away whenever he saw us going away, now leaped into the boat as soon as he saw us launching her. But what was our grief when we found two of our party missing; we had a thousand conjectures on the subject. Sometimes we thought they had fallen under the hands of the savages, others that they had hid themselves somewhere or were drowned trying to escape.

However we now kept constantly firing towards the cave hoping to shoot some of our enemies, & at the same time shouting to call our companions. In this manner, we lay till daylight, when one man went on shore, having first observed the beach was free from natives. He shortly afterwards returned with a look of dejection, followed by a flood of tears, in which we all joined, having a presentiment too true alas! of what had occurred.

This man found the boatsteerer laying by the fireside on his face, a corpse, one of his hands grasping a log of wood; his red flannel shirt was gathered about his breast covered in gory blood & his temples were cut across with some sharp weapon, so that his eyes were started. The other poor fellow was not to be found; we supposed they had carried him away dead or alive. One of our party said he recollected seeing a crowd of

Boultbee drew this sketch of a single and double hulled canoe around 1827.

qMS-257-01, Alexander Turnbull Library

natives striking at something on the ground & it is therefore likely it was the poor fellow alluded to, who was the very person who objected going away on the night of the catastrophe. The natives had evidently been confused, for their cockatoos [kākahu/cloaks] & spears were scattered about on the beach, & blood was seen in different places. They also had in their hurry, left several articles behind, such as bread, pork, a musket & a pair or two of trowsers. The greater part of the things however, they took away with them. Near the fire was convincing proofs of a desperate struggle having taken place, the firebrands were all scattered about, the fire had been extinguished by emptying our bucket of water on it, & the ground was turned up as if by the feet of persons engaged in a violent scuffle. ...

On bringing to mind what had transpired, I found I had much reason to be thankful for escaping not only from the natives, but also from being shot by my own companions: & it was a most extraordinary thing that I was not. They were about 12 yards from the boat, where they kept firing the musket; between them & the natives I stood engaged with my oar. At my back stood a man entirely unarmed, who could not get any weapon out of the boat; he it was who observed what we who were actively engaged were ignorant of. The natives had evinced no great resolution to continue their attack after the first onset, & had divided themselves in search of the plunder. One of our men panic struck on seeing we were unable to launch the boat, was about to run away, when his companion swore saying 'D—n your eyes! load & fire, or we are done, here are cartridges, & I will hand you them as fast as you can load.' This coolness & presence of mind saved us for even had we escaped these fellows, we should certainly have been killed sooner or later by other straggling savages. The man at my back said I was swearing & ranting all the time I was engaged. One thing was in my favour, — there was no wind or else I should not have been able to swing my oar in the manner I did, & I have since attempted to do it, but was not able, for at the time desperation served to create an unusual share of strength.

MUTINY AVERTED

CAPTAIN W.B. RHODES

William Barnard Rhodes (1807–78) was a sea captain and trader who later became an influential landowner in New Zealand. Born in Epworth, Lincolnshire, England, he went to sea at an early age and worked his way up — and around the world — on various ships. In 1836, he became master of the barque Australian. *Although inexperienced in whaling, he spent the next two years at that trade, working around New Zealand and the Pacific. Retiring from the sea in 1840, he settled in Wellington and became one of the leading merchants of the town and active in politics.*

Rhodes's whaling days are recalled in his journal for the years 1836–38, first published in 1954. Here is an account of a near-mutiny — a rebellion against authority — off the Canterbury coast in 1836.

August 2nd At 3 p.m. fastened to a large whale and killed her. Left her at anchor about 25 miles from the ship in harbour. The 4th Mate fastened to a whale and got stove. He anchored the stove boat and returned to the ship together with the crew in the 2nd Mate's boat at 11.30 p.m.

August 3rd At daylight, on turning the hands out to tow in the whale they refused, saying they were not able, being too much fatigued.

William Rhodes,
circa 1870s.

Photograph copied by Stanley
Polkinghorne Andrew,
1/1-018602-F, Alexander
Turnbull Library

I was therefore obliged very reluctantly to allow the whale to remain, together with the stove boat, at the great risk of losing both. However I thought it best to submit to the crew for once.

August 4th At 4 a.m. lowered four boats to go and tow in the whale. At 9 a.m., being in company with the Mate's boat saw whales. My boat was not furnished with lines or irons [harpoons]; I made a signal to the Mate to induce him to fasten, there being many whales round the boats, when to my great surprise he did not endeavour to do so, but remarked in very disrespectful language that it would be better to go and tow the dead whale. At 11.30 a.m. took the whale in tow with three boats, the other towing the stove boat. At 4.30 anchored the whale, being 20 miles from the ship. The Chief Mate and myself determined to remain all night by the whale. During the night the wind was fresh with a heavy sea, and our situation was not very comfortable at anchor in a whale boat during a cold night twenty miles from the land.

'Cutting in' a whale.
The ship is a barque,
as was the *Australian*
on which Rhodes
was the master.

The New Zealand Electronic
Text Collection

August 5th At daylight strong winds and cloudy. Found it impossible to tow the whale. At 9 very reluctantly left the whale at anchor and pull'd towards the harbour with a strong wind and heavy sea against us. At 10 the boat that returned to the ship came out again with provisions. At 7 p.m. arrived on board the ship pretty well fagg'd after been two days and a night exposed in a whale boat.

August 6th Strong breeze and squally weather. Boats not able to go out to tow in the whale. Lowered to go outside the heads, but being too much sea the boats returned. Midnight moderate.

August 7th At 6 a.m. I chanced to awake and immediately went on

Whaling terms

Captain Rhodes and his crew were engaged in **bay whaling**, where a whale ship would anchor near to shore, in some shelter, and small boats sent out to chase and kill whales. The carcases would then be brought back to the ship to be processed. Around the New Zealand coast, the bay whalers would mostly hunt right whales. Offshore, **pelagic whalers** chased sperm whales in deep waters to the north and east of New Zealand, and came into ports such as Kororāreka in the Bay of Islands to get provisions. Later, from the late 1820s, **shore whaling** stations were set up around the coast, also to target right and humpback whales as they migrated to and from the Pacific Ocean.

When bay whaling, whales would sometimes be killed many miles from the ship and have to be anchored, and then towed back over several days. **Fastened** means to harpoon a whale, and **stove** means the boat's hull was broken by the enraged mammal. **Hands** are the workers aboard the ship, and boats were **lowered** from the main ship's sides to pursue whales which had been spotted.

deck. I was surprised to find the hands had not been turned out, as orders had been given the night before to turn out at 5 to tow in the whale. Finding the cook on deck, I asked why he had not called me at 5 o'clock. He replied he had no orders, and was extremely abusive. Being irritated, I gave him a beating. Notwithstanding the noise made on deck none of the officers appeared. On going down the cabin to call the Chief Mate, I found him awake and in the act of turning out.

bursted rotted, the carcase falling apart

cutting in slicing the blubber off the whale

trying out melting down the blubber to get oil from it

On the hands being turned out they refused, and intimated they would do no more duty until a committee of captains was held on board on account of my conduct to the cook. This was a rather novel request. However I immediately [asked] the Mate to request the attendance of three captains from Port Cooper [Lyttelton]. Indeed I feel pleased at an opportunity of others witnessing the state of my crew.

At 10 a.m. the boat returned with Captain Howe of the *Harriet*, all the other captains having gone out a-whaling. The crew were then mustered, and after a good deal of desultory conversation, in which they appeared to take great umbrage at my having never been on a whaling voyage before, and said if only Mr Powel was allowed to be Whaling Master they would go to their duty, and no doubt they would make a good voyage. I told them by the advice of Captain Howe that I did not care what they called Mr Powel as long as they brought plenty of whales. They then went to their duty.

Capt. Howe observed that I had got an extremely rascally and mutinous set to deal with, and, not being supported properly by my officers, he plainly saw they were too lazy for black [right] whaling [*Eubalaena australis*], and advised me to go after sperm [whales, *Physeter macrocephalus*]. It had been my intention at daylight to muster the crew and inform them of my intention to get the ship under weigh and take her outside to pick up the whale, she being now 7 days old, and also to anchor the vessel outside, which, although it would be very dangerous, and at my risk should any accident occur, yet I was willing to risk the vessel to save them towing, provided they would exert themselves in future in procuring whales. . . .

August 8th Daylight moderate breeze and fine weather. At 8 a.m. saw whales; lowered after them. At 3 p.m. the ship picked up the dead whale and came to anchor in 20 fthms. water, Port Cooper bearing South, dist., about 7 leagues, off shore about three or four leagues.

August 9th Strong breeze and cloudy. At 7.30 a.m. commenced cutting in the whale. She was bursted, and in fact a complete wreck. Had we got her fresh she would have made 9 tons [of oil]; as it was she only made 4 after having had not a little trouble with her. On an average there is always 5 to 8 men off duty on pretence of being sick. At 8 p.m. commenced trying out part of the blubber, the whale being secured alongside.

August 10th At daylight began to cut in the remainder of the whale. At 2 p.m. finished cutting in the whale, having been nearly two days over it. Lowered two boats to go in search of the stove boat. At 8 p.m. the boats returned not having seen anything of the stove boat. I imagine she must have gone adrift during the late bad weather.

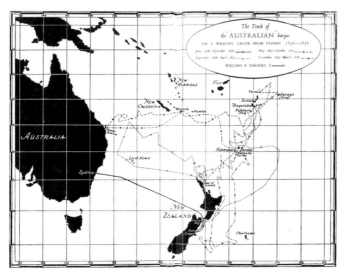

The track of the *Australian* on different whaling cruises it took between 1836 and 1838.

The New Zealand Electronic Text Collection

THE WHALERS OF TE-AWA-ITI

EDWARD JERNINGHAM WAKEFIELD

Edward Jerningham Wakefield (1820–79) was only 19 when he came to New Zealand with his uncle William Wakefield to help establish the settlements of the New Zealand Company. Edward Jerningham was the only son of Edward Gibbon Wakefield, founder of the Wakefield system of colonisation, which endeavoured to transfer a slice of British society to New Zealand to form a new country. Edward Jerningham Wakefield's visit to Te Awaiti on Arapawa [Arapaoa] Island at the outer edge of the Marlborough Sounds inspired this description of the 'shore whalers' who were among the first permanent settlers in New Zealand.

September 1 [1839], Sunday After prayers on board, we landed and visited the whaling-town of Te-awa-iti. Dicky Barrett's house was on a knoll at the far end of it, and overlooked the whole settlement and anchorage. There were about twenty houses presented to our view; the walls generally constructed of wattled supple-jack, called kareao, filled in with clay; the roof thatched with reeds; and a large unsightly chimney at one of the ends, constructed either of the same materials as the walls, or

The opening pages of Wakefield's diary.

of stones heaped together by rude masonry. Dicky Barrett's house, or ware [whare] as it is called in Maori or native language, was a very superior edifice built of sawn timber, floored and lined inside, and sheltered in front by an ample veranda. A long room was half full of natives and whalers. His wife E Rangi, a fine stately woman, gave us a dignified welcome; and his pretty half-caste [half-Māori] children laughed and commented on our appearance, to some of their mother's relations, in their own language. He had three girls of his own, and had adopted a son of an old trader and friend of his named Jacky Love, who was on his death-bed, regretted by the natives as one of themselves. He had married a young chieftainess of great rank, and his son Dan was treated with that universal respect and kindness to which he was entitled by the character of his father and the rank of his mother.

Edward Wakefield, circa 1860.

E.J. Wakefield, M.H.R., circa 1860, maker unknown. Purchased 1916. Te Papa (O.013579)

We found Williams's ware in the centre of the town; and Arthur's perched up on a pretty terrace on the side of the northern hill which slopes from the valley. A nice clear stream runs through the middle of the settlement. Some few of the whalers were dressed out in their clean Sunday clothes: but a large gang were busy at the try-works, boiling out the oil from the blubber of a whale lately caught. It appears that this is a process in which any delay is injurious. The try-works are large iron boilers, with furnaces beneath. Into these the blubber is put, being cut into lumps of about two feet square, and the oil is boiled out. The residue is called the scrag, and serves to feed the fire. The oil is

Dicky Barrett and his wife Wakaiwa Rāwinia (Lavinia), or Rangi, photographed in later life.

ARC2002-221, Puke Ariki

then run into coolers, and finally into casks ready for shipping. The men were unshaven and uncombed, and their clothes covered with dirt and oil. Most of them were strong, muscular men ... On asking one whether they always worked on Sundays, he answered contemptuously, "Oh! Sunday never comes in this 'bay!'". An Australian aboriginal native was one of this greasy gang, and was spoken of as a good hand. The whole ground and beach about here was saturated with oil, and the stench of the carcasses and scraps of whale-flesh lying about in the bay was intolerable.

Another man, heading a whale party here, was nicknamed "Geordie Bolts." His real name was Joseph Toms; but being crippled in an encounter with a whale, he had the fame of never being able to face one since; hence the nom de guerre [assumed name]. His appearance was by no means so attractive as that of Barrett. Independently of the deformity arising from his unfortunate accident, he was of small stature and repulsive features. Nor had he acquired the same character for hospitality and kindness to either natives or fellow-countrymen, which we found universally accorded to Dicky. He was married to a near relation of Rauparaha [Te Rauparaha], and by means of this alliance maintained another whaling station at a harbour called Porirua, on the main [land] between the islands of Kapiti and Mana.

In a bay separated by a low tongue of land from the main valley of Te-awa-iti, we found another whaler named Jimmy Jackson, who had a snug little cove all to himself. He was positively equal in dimensions to Williams and Barrett both together. He gave us a hearty welcome; and never ceased talking from the moment we entered his house until we returned on board. We found him quite an original character,

The Arapawa pig is a feral breed of domestic pig found on Arapawa Island. The breed was apparently brought to the island by whalers of the Te Awaiti whaling station in 1827. This stamp was released in 2007 to celebrate the Chinese Year of the Pig.

who had something to say on every subject ... He had been, we found, ten years here, being one of the first settlers. He declared the Pelorus river to be an excellent place for a settlement; and offered to introduce my uncle to an old friend of his in Cloudy Bay, Jack Guard, who knew the native owners of that district, and who piloted the "Pelorus" in her trips about the Strait. . . .

Since 1831 . . . when whaling-ships began to resort to Cloudy Bay, Sydney merchants worked the stations there and at other places on the coast by means of agents. They paid nominally £10 per ton for

Currency of the time

These amounts are in pounds sterling, shillings (s) and pence (d), the official currency of Great Britain. One pound was divided into 20 shillings, and one shilling was divided into 12 pennies.

In 1840, £10 would be roughly equivalent to £600 (NZ$1200) today, and £60 around £3600 (NZ$7000) today, so whale oil and bone (baleen) were valuable commodities. Wakefield estimated that the New Zealand whaling stations were producing 1200 tons of oil a year in the late 1830s.

The whaler's wage of £35 for a five-month season would be equal to around £2000 today — about the same as a skilled tradesman in England could earn in the same time, and more than an unskilled labourer would earn in a year. Wakefield notes that men with skills and trades, such as carpenters and blacksmiths, were better paid, earning 10 shillings (the equivalent of £30/NZ$60 today) per day, about twice what the whalers were earning.

A pound (2.2 kg) of tobacco for smoking would cost the equivalent of around £4 (NZ$8) in Sydney, but the whalers would be forced to pay £15 (NZ$30) or even £22 (NZ$45) for it at an isolated whaling station in New Zealand.

Whalers killing a sperm whale.

Duncan, Edward, 1803–82, Illustrated London News, PUBL-0033-1847-328, Alexander Turnbull Library

the oil, and £60 per ton for the bone, finding casks and freight themselves. The wages of the whalers, however, were paid in slops, spirits, and tobacco, at an exorbitant profit. A pound of tobacco, worth 1s. 3d. in Sydney, was valued at 5s. and sometimes 7s. 6d. here, and other things in the same proportion. The men, a mixture of runaway sailors and escaped convicts, sign an agreement at the beginning of the season, in which these prices are stated, so that they cannot go elsewhere to work, and must submit to these terms. The season lasts from the first of May to the beginning of October. In those five months, a whaler can earn £35 if the season be good; but all depends on the success of the fishery; as, if there were no whales caught, there would be no pay, and the only wages consist in a share of the produce. The consequence is a great number of bad debts in a bad season, and these fall on the agent or head of the party. If he does not advance the men what goods they want, they refuse to work; and sometimes have no means of paying their account at the end of the season.

The artisans seem to be the best off. Carpenters and blacksmiths get 10s. a day, and insist upon payment in money. Williams had amassed a good deal in this way, and having laid it out in purchasing goods of all sorts from whale-ships, he drove a good trade on shore, knowing whom to trust.

We were told that the different whaling parties on both shores of Cook Strait, near Banks Peninsula, and still further south, were reckoned to procure 1200 tons of oil annually, and that about 500 white men were employed in the pursuit.

The more industrious of these, during the summer, procure supplies of pigs and potatoes from the natives, and make large profits by disposing of them again to the whale-ships which look in at the different harbours previous to going out on the whaling-grounds, or returning home full. The less active spend the summer at the villages of their native women, either cultivating a patch of ground which the natives have tacitly allowed them to take possession of, or depending entirely on their native connexions for fish and potatoes, and drinking out the extent of their credit with the agent in the strongest and most poisonous liquors. . . .

The law of the strong in mind and body was, however, in force. Some few men of iron will and large limb ruled to a considerable degree the lawless assemblage, and maintained a powerful influence by their known courage and prowess, whether in the whale-boat or the fight on shore. Some few, too, though very few, like Dicky Barrett, were respected for their kindheartedness to all; and these, of better mould than the great body, expressed anxiety for the accomplishment of our objects.

The redeeming quality of hospitality we found unbounded among them; a stranger was always welcome to a share of the meal, a drop of the grog, and a seat on a stool, made of a whale's vertebra, in the ample chimney corner.

LIFE AMONG MĀORI

THE TATTOOED SAILOR

JOHN RUTHERFORD

John Rutherford, who called himself the White Chief or Tattooed Sailor, claimed to have been shipwrecked on the North Island east coast, possibly inside the Coromandel Peninsula, in the 1810s. On his return to Britain, having lived for ten years among Māori, he exhibited himself as a 'tattooed Englishman', and told colourful tales of his life in New Zealand, including being made a chief, two marriages and his final escape in 1823. Although the details may be exaggerated, his tales, first told in George Lillie Craik's The New Zealanders *in 1833, have some ring of truth, as he details Maori customs and life. Here he describes the process of being tattooed.*

The whole of the natives having then seated themselves on the ground in a ring, we were brought into the middle and, being stripped of our clothes, and laid on our backs, we were each of us held down by five or six men, while two others commenced the operation of tattooing us.

Having taken a piece of charcoal, and rubbed it upon a stone with a little water until they had produced a thickish liquid, they then dipped into it an instrument made of bone, having a sharp edge like a chisel, and shaped in the fashion of a garden-hoe, and immediately applied it to the skin, striking it twice or thrice with a small piece of wood. This made it cut into the flesh as a knife would

John Rutherford, from an original drawing made in 1828. The facial design is Māori but the chest tattoos look more like sailors' symbols and the stomach pattern is of another Pacific design.

have done, and caused a great deal of blood to flow, which they kept wiping off with the side of the hand, in order to see if the impression was sufficiently clear. When it was not, they applied the bone a second time to the same place. They employed, however, various instruments in the course of the operation; one of which they sometimes used being made of a shark's tooth, and another having teeth like a saw. They had them also of different sizes, to suit the different parts of the work.

While I was undergoing this operation, although the pain was most acute, I never either moved or uttered a sound; but my comrades moaned dreadfully. Although the operators were very quick and dextrous, I was four hours under their hands; and during the operation Aimy's [the chief's] eldest daughter several times wiped the blood from my face with some dressed flax. After it was over she led me to the river, that I might wash myself, for it had made me completely blind, and then conducted me to a great fire. They now returned us all our clothes, with the exception of our shirts, which the women kept for themselves, wearing them, as we observed, with the fronts behind.

A Māori warrior under the hands of the tribal tattooist at Te Uru Pā, 1906.

AWNS-19061227-13-1, Auckland Libraries Heritage Collections

We were now not only tattooed, but what they called tabooed [tapu], the meaning of which is, made sacred, or forbidden to touch any provisions of any kind with our hands. This state of things lasted for three days, during which time we were fed by the daughters of the chiefs, with the same victuals, and out of the same baskets, as the chiefs themselves, and the persons who had tattooed us. In three days, the swelling which had been produced by the operation had greatly subsided, and I began to recover my sight; but it was six weeks before I was completely well. I had no medical assistance of any kind during my illness; but Aimy's two daughters were very attentive to me, and would frequently sit beside me, and talk to me in their language, of which, as yet, however, I did not understand much.

Tā moko

Tā moko or tattooing was a significant feature of Māori culture, and fascinated the European travellers who saw it here and in the Pacific. Patterns carved into the skin with bone uhi (chisels) were coloured with pigment made from charcoal mixed with oil or liquid from plants. The process was carried out by highly skilled tohunga tā moko (tattoo experts), and was surrounded by ritual and tapu. Moko reflected a person's mana (status), so it was significant that Rutherford was tattooed by the tribe he lived with.

THREAT AND FIRE

AUGUSTUS EARLE

Paintings made by early visitors to New Zealand provided visual evidence of the new land, much as photography might do today. Augustus Earle (1793–1838) was a professional artist who worked in the Mediterranean and South America before finding his way to Australia, and then New Zealand in 1827. Based in Kororāreka, now Russell, in the Bay of Islands, Earle painted in the region for six months. At this time, the town was known as a 'hell-hole', in which whalers, traders and escaped convicts from around the world gathered, in a lawless and often violent community, at the mercy of their Māori hosts. This extract tells of a muru (plundering) raid on the Māori and Europeans of the town by a rival group seeking ritual compensation for a wrongdoing.

I was roused one morning at daybreak by my servant running in with the intelligence that a great number of war canoes were crossing the bay. As King George [Te Whareumu] had told us but the evening before that he expected a visit from Ta-ri-ah, a chief of the tribe called the Narpooes [Ngāpuhi], whose territory lay on the opposite side of the bay, and given us to understand that Ta-ri-ah [Ngāti Rēhia chief Tāreha] was a man not to be trusted, and therefore feared some mischief might happen if he really came, the sight of these war canoes naturally caused us considerable alarm, and we sincerely wished that the visit was over.

We dressed ourselves with the utmost expedition, and walked down to the beach. The landing of these warriors was conducted with a considerable degree of order; and could I have divested myself of all idea of danger, I should have admired the sight excessively. All our New Zealand friends — the tribe of Shulitea [Te Whareumu or 'King George'] — were stripped naked, their bodies were oiled, and all were completely armed; their muskets were loaded, their cartouch boxes [holding ammunition] were fastened round their waists, and their patoo-patoos [patu, small hand-held clubs] were fixed to their wrists. Their hair was tied up in a tight knot at the top of their heads, beautifully ornamented with feathers of the albatross. As the opposite party landed, ours all crouched on the ground, their eyes fixed on their visiters, and perfectly silent. When the debarkation was completed, I observed the chief Ta-ri-ah, put himself at their head, and march towards us with his party formed closely and compactly,

'King George', Te Whareumu, is second from left. He holds a taiaha (fighting staff) and is dressed in a traditional korowai (cloak).

Rex Nan Kivell Collection, NK12/84, National Library of Australia

Entrance to the
Bay of Islands,
painted in 1827, by
Augustus Earle.

Rex Nan Kivell Collection, NK12/66,
National Library of Australia

and armed with muskets and paddles. When they came very near, they suddenly stopped. Our party continued mute, with their firelocks [muskets] poised ready for use. For the space of a few minutes all was still, each party glaring fiercely on the other; and they certainly formed one of the most beautiful and extraordinary pictures I had ever beheld. The fore ground was formed by a line of naked savages, each resting on one knee, with musket advanced; their gaze fixed on the opposite party; their fine broad muscular backs contrasting with the dark foliage in front, and catching the gleam of the rising sun. The strangers were clothed in the most grotesque manner imaginable; some armed, some naked, some with long beards, others were painted all over with red ochre [clay]: every part of each figure was quite still, except the rolling and flaring of their eyes on their opponents. The background was formed by the beach, and a number of their beautiful war canoes dancing on the waves; while, in the distance, the mountains on the opposite side of the bay were just tinged with the varied and beautiful colours of the sun, then rising in splendour from behind them.

The stillness of this extraordinary scene did not last long. The Narpooes commenced a noisy and discordant song and dance, yelling, jumping, and making the most hideous faces. This was soon answered by a loud shout from our party, who endeavoured to outdo the Narpooes in making horrible distortions of their countenances: then succeeded another dance from our visiters; after which our friends made a rush, and in a sort of rough joke set them running. Then all joined in a pell-mell sort of encounter, in which numerous hard blows were given and received; then all the party fired their pieces [guns] in the air, and the ceremony of

'Two New Zealanders squatting'. The men in Earle's picture are holding muskets.

Rex Nan Kivell Collection, NK12/165, National Library of Australia

landing was thus deemed completed. They then approached each other, and began rubbing noses; and those who were particular friends cried and lamented over each other.

The slaves now commenced the labour of making fires to cook the morning meal, while the chiefs, squatting down, formed a ring, or rather an oblong circle, on the ground: then one at a time rose up, and made long speeches; which they did in a manner peculiar to themselves. The speaker, during his harangue, keeps running backwards and forwards within the oblong space, using the most violent but appropriate gesticulation; so expressive, indeed of the subject on which he is speaking, that a spectator, who does not understand the language, can form a tolerable idea as to what the affair is then under debate. The orator is never interrupted in his speech; but when he finishes and sits down, another immediately rises up and takes his place, so that all who choose have an opportunity of delivering their sentiments; after which the assembly breaks up.

Though the meeting of these hostile tribes had thus ended more amicably than King George and his party could have expected, it was easily to be perceived that the Narpooes were determined on executing some atrocity or depredations before their return; they accordingly pretended to recollect some old offence committed by the English settlers at the other end of the beach. They then marched to the residence of an English captain (who was in England), and plundered it of every thing that could be taken away; and afterwards sent us word that they intended to return to our end of the beach. Our fears were greatly increased by finding that our friends were not sufficiently strong to protect us from the superior force of the Narpooes; and our chief, George, being himself (we supposed) conscious of his inability, had left us to depend upon our own resources.

We now called a council of war of all the Europeans settled here; and it was unanimously resolved that we should protect and defend our houses and property, and fortify our position in the best way we could. Captain [Robert] Duke had in his possession four twelve-pounders [small cannons], and these we brought in front of the enclosure in which our huts were situated; and were all entirely employed in loading them with round and grape shot [types of ammunition], and had made them all ready for action, when, to our consternation and dismay, we found we had a new and totally unexpected enemy to contend with. By some accident one of our houses was in flames. Our situation was now perilous in the extreme. The buildings, the work of English carpenters, were constructed of dry rushes and well-seasoned wood; and this was one of a very respectable size, and we had hoped, in a very few days, would be finished fit for our removing into.

For some seconds we stood in mute amazement, not knowing to which point to direct our energies. As the cry of 'fire' was raised, groups of natives came rushing from all directions upon our devoted settlement, stripping off their

'The residence of Shulitea chief of Kororadika Bay of Islands, New Zealand', painted by Earle in 1827. Te Whareumu is with two women and a child.

Rex Nan Kivell Collection, NK12/75, National Library of Australia

clothes, and yelling in the most discordant pitch of voice. I entered the house, and brought out one of my trunks; but on attempting to return a second time I found it filled with naked savages, tearing every thing to pieces, and carrying away whatever they could lay their hands upon. The fierce raging of the flames, the heat from the fire, the yells of the men, and the shrill cries of the women, formed, altogether, a horrible combination: added to all this was the mortification of seeing all our property carried off in different directions, without the least possibility of our preventing it. The tribe of the Narpooes (who, when the fire began, were at the other end of the beach) left their operations in that quarter, and poured down upon us to share in the general plunder. Never shall I forget the countenance of the chief, as he rushed forward at the head of his destroying crew! He was called 'The Giant;' and he was well worthy of the name, being the tallest and largest man I had ever seen: he had an immense bushy black beard; and grinned exultingly when he saw the work of destruction proceeding with such rapidity and kept shouting loudly to his party to excite them to carry off all they could.

Tāreha

Tāreha was a significant leader in several parts of the Bay of Islands in the early 1800s, and other observers also recorded his size: missionary Richard Taylor wrote that the chief was nearly 7 feet (2.1 metres) tall. By contrast, the average Englishman of that time was around 5 feet 5 inches (1.65 metres).

A cask containing seventy gallons of rum now caught fire and blew up with a terrible explosion; and the wind freshening considerably, huge volumes of smoke and flame burst out in every direction. Two of our houses were so completely enveloped, that we had given up all hopes of saving them. The third, which was a beautifully carved taboo'd [tapu] one, some little distance from the others, and which we had converted into a store and magazine, was now the only object of our solicitude and terror. For, besides the valuable property of various kinds which were deposited within it, it contained several barrels of gunpowder! It was in vain we attempted to warn the frantic natives to retire from the vicinity of this danger. At length we persuaded about a dozen of the most rational to listen while we explained to them the cause of our alarm; and they ascended to the roof, where, with the utmost intrepidity and coolness, they kept pouring water over the thatch, thus lessening the probability of an immediate explosion. About this time we noticed the re-appearance of King George; which circumstance rekindled our hopes. He was armed with a thick stick, which he laid heavily on the backs of such of his subjects as were running away with our property; thus forcing them to relinquish their prizes, and to lay them down before his own mansion, where all was safe. By this means a great deal was re-collected. The fire was now nearly extinguished; but our two really tolerably good houses were reduced to a heap of smoking ruins, and the greater part of what belonged to us was taken away by the Narpooes.

THE ARRIVAL OF 'DOUBTFUL FRIENDS'

F.E. MANING

Frederick Edward Maning (1811–83) was a young adventurer who used the knowledge he gained living among Māori to become a respected judge with the Maori Land Court in later life. Maning came to New Zealand in 1833, at the age of 22, and settled first at Kohukohu on the Hokianga Harbour, working as a small-scale trader and contractor. He later operated a store, and moved into the timber and gum trade in the late 1840s. When Judge Maning came to publish his account of 'Old New Zealand' in 1863, he wrote under the name of 'A Pakeha Maori.' Here he describes the return of a war expedition to the Hokianga , led by Ngāpuhi warrior chief Tītore, nephew of Tāreha, in 1833. Maning's account is not necessarily accurate, but it is a colourful and exciting story.

Towards evening a messenger from a neighbouring friendly tribe arrived to say that next day, about noon, the strangers might be expected; and also that the peace which had concluded with their tribe during their absence had been ratified and accepted by them. This was satisfactory intelligence; but, nevertheless, no precaution must be neglected. To be thrown off guard would invite attack, and ensure destruction; everything must be in order; gun cleaning, flint fixing, cartridge making, was going on in all directions; and the outpost at the edge of the forest was not called in. All was active preparation.

The path by which these doubtful friends were coming led through a dense forest and came out on the clear plain about half a mile from the pa, which plain continued and extended in every direction around the fortress to about the same distance, so that none could approach unperceived. The outpost of twenty men were stationed at about a couple of hundred yards from the point where the path emerged from the wood; and as the ground sloped considerably from the forest to the fort, the whole intervening space was clearly visible.

Judge F.E. Maning, in later life.

Grey Collection, Auckland Libraries Heritage Collection

Another night of alarm and sleepless expectation, the melancholy moan of the tetere [tētere, trumpet made from flax leaves] still continuing to hint to any lurking enemy that we were all wide awake; or rather, I should say, to assure him most positively of it, for who could sleep with that diabolical din in his ears? Morning came, and an early breakfast was cooked and devoured hurriedly. Then groups of the younger men might be seen here and there fully armed, and 'getting up steam' by dancing the war dance, in anticipation of the grand dance of the whole warrior force of the tribe, which, as a matter of course, must be performed in honour of the visitors when they arrived. In honour, but quite as much in intimidation, or an endeavour at it, though no one said so. Noon arrived at last. Anxious glances are turning from all quarters towards the wood, from which a path is plainly seen winding down the sloping ground towards the pa. The outpost is on the alert. Straggling scouts are out in

The inside of a pā,
circa 1852.

Gilfillan, John. Gift of Horace
Fildes, 1937. Te Papa
(1992-0035-1744)

every direction. All is expectation. Now there is a movement at the outpost. They suddenly spread in an open line, ten yards between each man. One man comes at full speed running towards the pa, jumping and bounding over every impediment. Now something moves in the border of the forest — it is a mass of black heads. Now the men are plainly visible. The whole taua [war party] has emerged upon the plain. 'Here they come! Here they come!' is heard in all directions. Then men of the outpost cross the line of march in pretended resistance; they present their guns, make horrid grimaces, dance about like mad baboons, and then fall back with headlong speed to the next advantageous position for making a stand. The taua, however, comes on steadily; they are formed in a solid oblong mass. The chief at the left of the column leads them on. The men are all equipped for immediate action — that is to say, quite naked except their arms and cartridge boxes, which are a warrior's clothes. No one can possibly tell what this peaceful meeting may end in, so all are ready for action at a second's notice. The taua still comes steadily on. As I have said, the men are all stripped for action, but I also notice that the appearance of nakedness is completely taken away by the tattooing, the colour of the skin, and the arms and equipments. The men in fact look much better than when dressed in their Maori clothing. Every man, almost without exception, is covered with tattooing from the knees to the waist; the face is also covered with dark spiral lines. Each man has round his middle a belt, to which are fastened two cartridge boxes, one behind and one before; another belt goes over the right shoulder and under the left arm, and from it hangs, on the left side and rather behind, another cartridge box, and under the waist belt is thrust behind, at the small of the back, a short-handled tomahawk for close fight and to finish the wounded. Each cartridge box contains eighteen rounds, and every man has a musket. Altogether this taua is better and more uniformly armed and equipped than ordinary; but they have been amongst the first who got pakehas to trade with them, and are indeed, in consequence, the terror of New Zealand. On they come, a set of tall, athletic heavy-made men; they would, I am sure, in the aggregate weigh some tons heavier than the same number of men taken at random from the streets of our manufacturing towns. They are now half-way across the plain; they keep their formation, a solid oblong, admirably as they advance, but they do not keep step; this causes a very singular appearance when distant. Instead of the regular marching step of civilized soldiers, which may be observed at any distance, this mass seems to progress towards you with the creeping motion of some great reptile, and when coming down a sloping ground this effect is quite remarkable.

The mimic opposition is now discontinued; the outpost rushes in at full speed, the men firing their guns in the air as they run.

An early 1840s portrayal of traditional Māori weapons, superseded by the arrival of the musket.

Angas, George, 1822–86, PUBL-0014-58, Alexander Turnbull Library

Takini! Takini! is the cry, and out spring three young men, the best runners of our tribe, to perform the ceremony of the taki [wero, ritual challenge]. They hold in their hands some reeds to represent darts or kokiri. At this moment a tremendous fire of ball cartridge opens from the fort; the balls whistle in every direction, over and around the advancing party, who steadily and gravely come on, not seeming to know that a gun has been fired, though they perfectly well understand that this salute is also a hint of full preparation for any unexpected turn things may take. Now, from the whole female population arises the shrill 'Haere mai! Haere mai! [call of welcome]' Mats are waving, guns firing, dogs barking; the chief roaring to 'fall in', and form for the war dance. He appears half-mad with excitement, anxiety, and something very like apprehension of a sudden onslaught from his friends. In the midst of this horrible uproar off dart three runners. They are not unexpected. Three young men of the taua are seen to tighten their waist-belts and hand their muskets to their comrades. On go the three young men from the fort. They approach the front of the advancing column; they dance and caper about like mad monkeys, twisting their faces about in the most extraordinary manner, showing the whites of their eyes, and lolling out their tongues. At last, after several feints, they boldly advance within twenty yards of the supposed enemy, and send the reed darts flying full in their faces; then they turn and fly as if for life. Instantly, from the stranger ranks, three young men dart forth in eager pursuit; and behind them comes the solid column, rushing on at full speed. Run now, O 'Sounding Sea' (Tai Haruru), for the 'Black Cloud' (Kapua Mangu), the swiftest of the Rarawa, is at your back; run now, for the honour of your tribe and your own name, run! run! It was an exciting scene.

The two famous runners came on at a tremendous pace, the dark mass of armed men following close behind at full speed, keeping their formation admirably, the ground shaking under them as they rushed on. On come the two runners (the others are left behind and disregarded). The pursuer gains upon his man; but they are fast nearing the goal, where, according to Maori custom, the chase must end. Run 'Sounding Sea'! Another effort! Your tribe are near in full array, and armed for the war dance; their friendly ranks are your refuge; run! run! On came the headlong race. When within about thirty yards of the place where our tribe was now formed in a solid oblong, each man kneeling on one knee, with musket held in both hands, butt to the ground, and somewhat sloped to the front, the pursuing native caught at the shoulder of our man, touched it, but could do no more. He will, however, boast everywhere that he has touched the shoulder of the famous 'Sounding Sea'. Our man has not, however, been caught, which would have been a bad omen. At this moment the charging column come thundering up to where their man is standing; instantly they all kneel upon one knee, holding their guns sloped before their faces in the manner already described. The elite of the two tribes are now opposite to each other, all armed, all kneeling, and formed in two solid oblong masses, the narrow end of the oblong to the front. Only thirty yards divide them; the front ranks do not gaze on each other; both parties turn their eyes towards the ground, and with heads bent downwards, and a little to one side, appear to listen. All in silence; you might have heard a pin drop. The uproar has turned to a calm; the men are kneeling statues; the chiefs have disappeared — they are in the centre of their tribes. The pakeha is beginning to wonder what will be the end of all this and also to speculate on the efficacy of the buckshot with which his gun is loaded, and wishes it was ball. Two minutes have elapsed in this solemn silence, the more remarkable as being the first quiet two minutes for the last two days and nights. Suddenly from the extreme rear of the strangers' column is heard a scream — a horrid yell. A savage of herculean stature, comes, mere [flat hand-held weapon] in hand, rushing madly to the front. He seems hunted by all the furies. Bedlam never produced so horrid a visage. Thrice, as he advances, he gives that horrid cry, and thrice the armed tribe give answer with a long-drawn gasping sigh. He is at the front; he jumps into the air, shaking his stone weapon; the whites only of his eyes are visible, giving a most hideous appearance to his face; he shouts the first words of the war song, and instantly his tribe spring from the ground. It would be hard to describe the scene that followed. The roaring chorus of the war song; the horrid grimaces; the eyes all white; the tongues hanging out; the furious yet measured and uniform gesticulation, jumping, and stamping. I felt the ground plainly trembling. At last the war dance ended; and then my tribe (I find I am already beginning to get Maorified), starting from the ground like a single man, endeavoured to out-do even their amiable friends' exhibition. They end; then the newcomers perform another demon dance; then my tribe give another. Silence again prevails, and all sit down. Immediately a man from the new arrivals comes to the front of his own party; he runs to and fro; he speaks for his tribe; these are his words: 'Peace is made! peace is made; peace is firm! peace is secure! peace! peace! peace!'

A portrayal of a haka, painted in 1836.

PUBL-0014-53, Angas, George French, 1822–86, Alexander Turnbull Library

STRANGE JOURNEYS

IN THE FOOTSTEPS OF COOK

JOEL POLACK

Joel Samuel Polack (1807–82) was born in London, England, the son of immigrant Jews. He worked and travelled in South Africa, North America and Australia before arriving in New Zealand and setting up business as a trader in the Hokianga, then the Bay of Islands. Polack returned to England in 1838, where he gave evidence before the Select Committee of the House of Lords, advocating the colonisation of New Zealand. The first of his two books, New Zealand, being a Narrative of Travels and Adventures, *was published at this time.*

This account from June 1835 describes visiting Tolaga Bay (Ūawa) on the East Cape, where Captain James Cook made landfall in 1769.

We were apprised of the Chief Kani [Te Kani-ā-Takirau, of Te Aitanga-a-Hauiti of Ngāti Porou], and his retinue of warriors, by a loud report of musketry in the southern village. . . . Advancing up to me, we pressed noses, (ongi [hongi]) and entered into conversation, regretting he had not been at home on my arrival, to prevent any previous unpleasantness; that his absence at Turunga [Tūranga], (Poverty Bay) was occasioned by some quarrels that had broken out among some of the minor chiefs of that place, and those under his chieftainship; that detesting war himself, he had undertaken the journey with a few friendly warriors, to obtain a league of friendship with the opposite party, and had been fortunate enough to succeed in his endeavours to allay the animosity that had then existed for some time.

. . . I assured him I had much longed for his arrival, and presented him with a small box containing several esteemed trifles, on the receipt of which, by an attendant (for the chief was tápued by the priest on his arrival, and dared not handle anything) he appeared much delighted. "Aroai de pakéha!" "Kaátai taku oá!" "A ná ná!" Exclamations of surprise and pleasure burst from the lips of the gratified man, as each article was produced, and held up to him. After discussing the usefulness of each to his admiring friends, he suddenly turned to them and said, "What can I give the white man who has treated me so well?" This equally posed the gentlemen in waiting, they appeared somewhat *hors de combat* [unable to act to injure or damage], when a young man who had attached himself to me, previously to

Accents

Polack used French-style accents to represent how Māori words sounded to him. Today we use macrons to indicate how vowels should be pronounced.

The European in this image is thought to be Joel Polack.

A-079-017, Alexander Turnbull Library

the arrival of Kani, said, "That the two spike nails originally given by Te Kuki (Cook) to the natives of Turunga, and captured in battle by Kani's father from the original possessor, would be most acceptable;" the chief sent on shore for them immediately. Kani then asked what could induce me to prize a couple of old nails, when I was giving away articles of infinitely greater value made of a similar material, and concluded by asking if Cook was my father or uncle. I told him, proud as I should be of the relationship, I could not boast of being so nearly connected, but that I belonged to the same tribe of Europeans, and was born under the same venerable chieftain; he than asked if Kuki had been a great chief in his own country Ingéráni [Ingarani] (England). I answered that no name was held in greater estimation, and that the benefit he did his tribe in making known to them countries, the existence of which they were previously to his time ignorant, would cause his services to be cherished by future tribes yet unborn.

By this time the envoy who had been sent for the nails, returned bringing also with him two handsome garments or mats (kaitáká) [kaitaka, fine flax cloak] made of dressed silken flax; the nails were tied together with a piece of flax; one was a five inch spike without any head, (originally formed so) the other was a six inch spike with a small projection on the head, but not lapping over on each side: they had an antique appearance, and had been used by the natives as chisels, for carving boxes for their little trinkets. These, together with the mats, were thrown at my feet by the command of the chief, in the usual ungraceful manner, wherein these people are wont to make presents.

They were much surprised at the visible delight I displayed in gaining such valued relics of the greatest navigator, in whatever light we view him, that ever lived. Kani was also much pleased with the reception his presents had met with, and approaching his wife, who with some of her maidens were remarkably mirthful, sitting on the taffrail of the cutter [the stern of a small yacht], pointed to three light blue beads that were appended round her throat, with a piece of flax, said, that those, together with the nails were the

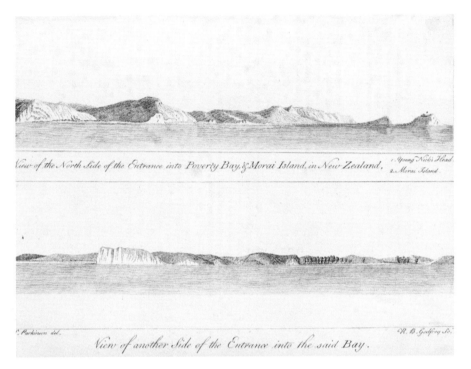

View of the North Side of the Entrance into Poverty Bay, & Morai Island, in New Zealand.   1. Young Nicks Head.
2. Morai Island.

C. Parkinson del.   R. B. Godfrey Sc.

View of another Side of the Entrance into the said Bay.

View of the mouth of the Turanganui River, Gisborne, 1835.

PUBL-0115-2-120, Alexander Turnbull Library

only relics left of the great Kuki; and from what I had said of him, and the delight I had felt on receiving the nails, should never be parted with out of his family.

The beads underwent an examination all round for the thousandth time, and anecdotes were repeated of that celebrated man and his Tahitian interpreter Tupia [Tupaia]; these kept us in conversation for some time. Our anecdote on the first introduction of gunpowder was somewhat laughable. A small quantity of that combustible material had been given to the native head chief (Kani's father) who, to his unpracticed eye, not perceiving any vast difference between it and the seeds the Europeans had planted, was delighted at the idea of a new vegetable food, to vary the monotonous edibles then only known in this country; — accordingly the natives were ordered by the chief, superintended by himself, to prepare in the most careful manner a plot of ground for this new légume [vegetable], that was to be indigenous for the future to the soil. The gunpowder was accordingly planted, after a smart shower had previously fallen, to ensure the fruition of the supposed seed; with what success need not be added; part of the stock was consumed by throwing small portions on the fire, the blazing of which surprised the people vastly; but one man, more impatient than the rest, threw the remaining quantity on the ashes, the effects of which, though the quantity was small, quickly dispersed the group exclaiming it was the "atua no to pákehá," (the Deity of the white man).

Kani requested me to accompany him next day to Opotoumu [Opoutama], near the south entrance of the bay, where we should walk

One of the images from Polack's book.

J.S. Polack's map of
New Zealand, which
he drew in 1838.

AAME 8106 W5603 120/
12/5/16, Archives New Zealand
Te Rua Mahara o te Kāwanatanga

over the same ground, and native paths that
existed in the time of Cook, and which had
been traversed by him. . . . Cook calls this place
Tolaga Bay, which is evidently a misnomer as
the word is unpronounceable by many of the
New Zealanders; the place is termed by the
natives Ou Auwoa or Uwoua [Ūawa]. . . .

We had almost pulled [rowed] to our
destination, when we arrived opposite to a very
large cavern, very high and of some depth; we

did not stay long to admire this natural curiosity, as close adjoining it, a splendid perforated natural arch burst on our view, exceeding in grandeur anything of the kind I had ever beheld; a reef of rocks ran out into the bay from this gigantic causeway; it was of argillaceous [clay] formation similar to the cliffs around. Here I requested to land, which we accordingly did, the perforation led into a valley. I employed some time in sketching this magnificent curiosity, during which the natives made their remarks on the progress of the drawing, one proposing such an alteration, which I no sooner complied with, than not a little laughter ensued at the taste displayed by the scrutinizing eye of my Mentor.

The appearance of either side of the arch was romantic in the extreme: shrubs and small trees of every description peculiar to these parts, hung in wild luxuriance from crevices among the rocks; but the mind will scarcely conceive the awful tempests, whose repeated ravages could have battered so large an opening in these cliffs.

Through the valley we reached the indent of Opotoumu, beautifully situated in a dell, encircled by rising hills covered in a variety of shrubby trees, evergreens that appeared equally beautiful now in depth of winter, as in the more genial season of summer; not a leaflet but bore the liveliest hue. . . .

The chief now wound his way up the side of the hill followed by myself and the friends who accompanied us. We were arrested in our progress half way by a cavern, (háná,) [ana] which stopt our farther progress. Its arch was remarkably high, but of little depth; it was similarly argillaceous as the caves we had seen below in the bay. Kani enquired if I felt gratified, adding "Ekoro, tenei ano te háná no Tupia," [E hoa, ko te ana tēnei o Tupaia] (this, friend, is Tupia's cavern.) I learnt that in this cave the favourite interpreter of Cook slept with the natives: "he was often in the habit of doing so during the heats of the day with his native friends, as is the wont of the New Zealanders," said my conductor; "Tupia was a great favourite with our fathers, so much so, that to gratify him, several children who were born in the village, during his sojourn among us, were named after him." A few yards in front of the cave, is a small hole that was dug in the granite rock, by order of Cook, for receiving from a small spring, the fluid that unceasingly flows into it. The marks of the pick axe are as visible, at the present day, as at the period it was excavated under Cook's eye. The water that overflowed this useful little memorial of our illustrious countryman, was pellucid and very cold. The sun had not penetrated this sequestered spot, for many years, from the umbrageous [shady] kaikátoa [kahikatea], and other trees that surround it.

Around the surface of the cavern are many native delineations, executed with charcoal of ships, canoes sailing, men and women, dogs and pigs, and some obscenities drawn with tolerable accuracy. Above our reach, and evidently faded by time, was the representation of a ship and some boats, which were unanimously pointed out to me, by all present, as the productions of the faithful Tahitian follower of Cook, (Tupia.) This also had evidently been done by similar materials. This cavern is made use of as a native resting place for the night, as the villages of Uwoua are at some considerable distance from Opotoumu; it is mostly in request by parties fishing for the kohuda [kōura], (craw fish,) and other fish, which abound in all these bays, and of which an immense quantity is procurable in the vicinity.

I was much pleased with my excursion, and after a review of the beautiful and interesting localities, we entered the boat which had been sent round the bay to meet us. It has seldom been my lot to fall in with scenery more romantic than I found in this small bay of Opotoumu, enhanced by the cherished associations of the immortal circumnavigator.

ASCENT OF EGMONT

ERNST DIEFFENBACH

*Swiss-trained doctor Johann Karl Ernst Dieffenbach (1811–55) was
one of several experts hired by the New Zealand Company to advise it
on places to settle and the qualities of the new land. Although he was
a medical doctor, Dieffenbach was employed as a naturalist, exploring
widely in the North Island during 1839–40 and publishing a two-
volume book called* Travels in New Zealand *with contributions to the
Geography, Geology, Botany and Natural History of that Country.
Dieffenbach's ascent of what is now known as Mount Taranaki or Mount
Egmont, on Christmas Day 1839, is believed to be the first by a European.
Here he describes his second attempt to summit the mountain.*

During our absence plenty had reigned at Nga Motu [Ngā Motu/
Sugar Loaf Islands, at what is now Port Taranaki]: natives had gone
out fishing, and the quantity of
fish they took was so great, that
they were enabled to dry large
numbers in the sun for store.
Pigs and potatoes had also been
brought from the southward. A
Waikato chief, with his followers,
had come on a friendly visit from
Kawia [Kawhia], and there was

NEW ZEALAND COMPANY.
INCORPORATED BY ROYAL CHARTER, A.D. 1841.

Mt Taranaki, 1877.

New Zealand Graphic and Descriptive. Mt Egmont., 1877, London, by Charles Decimus Barraud, Elizabeth Walker, C F Kell, Sampson Low Marston Searle & Rivington. Te Papa (1988-0004-6)

apparently a good understanding between them and the natives at this place. The abundance of food enabled me to start again on the 19th, determined, at all hazards, to accomplish the ascent of the mountain. I persuaded E Kake [Te Kaki?], one of the chiefs, to accompany me, who took a slave with him, and sent on before a female slave to one of his plantations which lay in our route, with an order to prepare maize-cakes for us to carry as provisions. The companions of my last trip again accompanied me, and our party was joined by Mr. [James 'Worser'] Heberley, a European, who had come with us from Te-awa-iti [on Arapaoa Island in the Marlborough Sounds], where he had lived for several years as a whaler, and who was most expert in finding his way through all the difficulties attending such an expedition as this.

This time I was more fortunate. Although we

took a different route, in order to obtain provisions at the settlements of E Kake, in four days we reached our last halting-place at the foot of the mountain. We had to walk for some distance along the rocky bed and through the icy water of the Waiwakaio [Waiwhakaiho]; but notwithstanding the force of its rapid current, which often threatened to throw us down, we heeded not the difficulty, as we had the gratification of seeing the summit of the mountain directly before us. We climbed at last up a ridge rising on the left bank of the river, and running in a north-east direction from Mount Egmont. This ridge is very narrow, and forms, towards the river, a sharp escarpment; nor was it without some difficulty that we reached its crest. Higher up is a frightful precipice, close to the edge of which we had to walk. Lying down, we looked over into the deep gorge, which appeared to be split asunder by volcanic agency, and to have been hollowed out more and more by the action of the river. . . .

Not far from this point the ridge forms a platform, from which rises the pyramidical summit. We reached the platform by descending into a deep gorge which an arm of the Waiwakaio river has scooped out of the blue lava. We walked with ease in the rocky channel thus formed, and soon came to the source of this arm, which took its rise from under a frozen mass of snow which filled up the ravine and remained unmelted, although it was now the middle of summer. This place, however, is not to be regarded as lying within the limits of perpetual snow, as the duration of this frozen mass resulted from the fact that the influence of the sun was obstructed by high walls rising on both sides. . . . We now began to ascend the cone, which consisted of cinders, or slags of scoriaceous lava, of various colours — red, white, or brown, — and had been reduced almost to a gravel, so as to offer no resistance to our feet. ... We soon came to the snow, at a point about 1500 feet below the summit. ... Vegetation had long ceased, not from

Maunga

Dieffenbach was climbing the mountain against the wishes of local Māori. In Māori culture, mountains represent ancestors, and the summit is the head, the most sacred part of the body, so to stand on an ancestor's head is considered highly offensive.

the great elevation, but from the entire absence of even a patch of soil where plants might take root. In the ravines, as I have already observed, the snow was found much lower down.

As soon as we had reached the limits of perpetual snow, my two native attendants (the third had been left behind at the last night's halting-place) squatted down, took out their books, and began to pray. No native had ever before been so high, and, in addition to that awe which grand scenes of nature and the solemn silence reigning on such height produce in every mind, the savage views such scenes with superstitious dread. … My native attendants would not go any farther, not only on account of their superstitious fears, but because, from the intensity of the cold, their uncovered feet had already suffered severely. I started, therefore, for the summit, accompanied by Heberley alone. The slope of the snow was very steep, and we had to cut steps in it, as it was frozen on the surface. Higher up we found some support in large pieces of rugged scoriæ, which, however, increased the danger of the ascent, as they obstructed our path, which lay along a narrow ridge, while on both sides yawned an abyss filled with snow. However, we at length reached the summit, and found that it consisted of a field of snow about a square mile in extent. Some protruding blocks of scoriæ, of a reddish-brown colour, and here and there slightly vitrified [turned to volcanic glass] on the surface, indicated the former existence of an active volcano. A most extensive view opened before us, and our eye followed the line of coast towards Kawia and Waikato.

The country over which we looked was but slightly elevated; here and there broken, or with irregular ramifications of low hills, towards the snowy group of the Ruapahu [Ruapehu; the Tongariro volcanoes] in the interior, which bore N60°W. I had just time to look towards Cook's Straits and distinguish Entry Island [Kapiti], when a dense fog enveloped us, and prevented all further view. Whilst waiting in the hope that the fog would disperse, I tried the temperature of boiling-water with one of Newman's thermometers, and found it to be 197°, the temperature of the air being 49°, which, taking 55° as the mean of the temperatures

Mt Taranaki's height

Dieffenbach measured the temperature at which water boils to work out the height of the mountain. Water boils at 100°C at sea level, and at a lower temperature at higher altitudes. Elevation above sea level can be calculated from this. 197° Fahrenheit is around 92 degrees Celsius, 49°F = 9.4°C, and 55°C = 12.8°C.

Dieffenbach's calculations weren't far wrong: in fact, Mt Taranaki is 8261 feet (2518 metres) high.

TRAVELS
to
NEW ZEALAND;

WITH CONTRIBUTIONS TO THE
GEOGRAPHY, GEOLOGY, BOTANY, AND NATURAL
HISTORY OF THAT COUNTRY.

By ERNEST DIEFFENBACH, M.D.,
Late Naturalist to the New Zealand Company.

IN TWO VOLUMES.—VOL. I.

LONDON:
JOHN MURRAY, ALBEMARLE STREET.
1843.

The New Zealand Electronic
Text Collection

at the summit and the base, would give 8839 feet as the height of Mount Egmont. ...

After staying some time on the summit, in the vain hope that the clouds which enveloped us would disperse, we retraced our steps, and accomplished the descent with comparitive ease. The natives expressed their joy at seeing us again, as they had already given us up as lost. We encamped on the bank of the left branch of the Waiwakaio amidst trees of the *Leptospermum* [mānuka] species. ... In future times this picturesque valley, as well as Mount Egmont and the smiling open land at its base, will become as celebrated for their beauty as the Bay of Naples, and will attract travellers from all parts of the globe.

Manuka.

48/4/19, Hetley, Georgina,
Gifted by the Misses Hetley,
MTG Hawke's Bay

A GOLDEN DREAM

JOHN LOGAN CAMPBELL

John Logan Campbell (1817–1912) is best known as 'the father of Auckland'. This Scottish doctor settled on what became known as Browns Island (Motukorea) before the establishment of the town. Campbell came ashore to become a pioneer trader and brewer in the city, but at the time of this account Auckland was yet to be settled by Europeans. Campbell recalls walking over the site of the future city in 1840 in his memoir of the early days, Poenamu, *written in later life and published in 1881. His vision of the future practically coincides with the establishment of British government in New Zealand and the end of the lawless days.*

Beautiful was Remuera's wooded shore, sloping gently to Waitemata's [Waitematā] sunlit waters in the days of which I write. The palm fern-tree was there, with its crown of graceful bending fronds and black feathery-looking young shoots; and the karaka with its brilliantly-polished green leaves and golden yellow fruit; contrasting with the darker, crimped and varnished leaf of the puriri, with its bright cherry-like berry. Evergreen shrubs grew on all sides of every shade from palest to deepest green; lovely flowering creepers mounted high overhead, leaping from tree to tree and hanging in rich festoons; of beautiful ferns there was a profusion underfoot. The tui [tūī], with his grand rich note, made the wood musical; the great, fat, stupid pigeon [kererū] cooed

John Logan Campbell.

Yale Center for British Art,
Paul Mellon Collection

down upon you almost within reach, nor took the trouble to fly away. There was nothing to run away from us; for Nature, however prodigal in other respects, had not been so in vouchsafing any four-footed game.

But Tangata Maori's [the Māori people] transition epoch had already set in. He now sometimes donned a shirt under his blanket, though the restraint of a pair of inexpressibles [tight trousers] was still unknown to him and still a thing of the future. Pigs, thanks to circumnavigator Cook, were now plentiful in the land ... As for smoking, if a Maori had only tobacco enough his pipe was never out of his mouth, so he was making slow but very sure steps in the march of civilisation. And here we were deliberately planning to erect a town on the shore of the Waitemata, and thus place him in the very centre of seducing temptations, with the pure and disinterested motive of reclaiming him from his savagedom and hoping whilst doing so to receive our reward in the manner we wished. We were now in quest of the owners of the soil to see on what terms we could acquire it. We had not taken long to decide that Wepiha's [William Webster, an American trader living on an island in the Coromandel Harbour] praises of the Waitemata were not exaggerated, and on no more fitting shores could a township be located. And it appeared to us on that bright and lovely morning that no town could lie on a more beautiful spot than the slopes of that shore. As we gained the summit of the ridge and turned to look seaward we stood entranced at the panorama revealed — stood entranced

in mute amazement at the wonderful beauty of the glorious landscape.

Yes, we had come on this excursion site-hunting! We were going to purchase a modest tract of country and supply impatient intending settlers with town, suburban and country lands to their hearts' content, or rather to the extent that their purses would give power of paying. Castles in the air which we had been building of rapidly-amassed fortunes seemed to assume a palpable reality now that Wepiha had unfolded to us the grand and beautiful isthmus which we were now traversing. Well justified was he, truly, in having said at the Herekino *table d'hôte* [Webster's trading base on Whanganui

The campsite of the advance party sent to establish the newly founded city of Auckland in September 1840.

E-216-f-115, Alexander Turnbull Library

Island] in mysterious yet oracular tone, 'Wait until you see the Waitemata' — we came, we saw and were conquered. Without one dissentient word we succumbed; we now all swore by the Waitemata, and were jubilant exceedingly as we walked along the native footpath, the high fern and tupakihi [tūpākihi, tree tutu] proclaiming the richness of the soil. An hour's walk brought us to the base of a volcanic mount, some five hundred feet high, rising suddenly from the plain, the name of which Wepiha told us was Maungakiekie, but as it had one solitary large tree on its crater summit we christened it 'One Tree Hill', which forever obliterated the Maori name from Pakeha vocabulary, but the grand old tree has passed away, causing later-day arrivals to wonder why the hill bears its name. Alas that native names should have been replaced by Mount Eden [Maungawhau], Wellington [Maungarei], Hobson [Remuwera/Ōhinerau], Smart! [Rarotonga]— as if we were the smart people who would have changed them to Mount One, Two, and so on. And the islands in and around the harbour had better have been called A, B, C Islands, rather than change Motu-Korea to Brown's Island.

What a blessed thing that Rangitoto has escaped the sacrilege of being named forever as perhaps 'Two-Pap Peak Hill'! Had it been smitten with such an indignity the very name would have marred the beauty of that island's lovely outline, and the landscape would not have been the same with such hideous words paining the ear. ...

But I must retrace my steps to the base of Maungakiekie, and where we first looked down upon, and felt the fresh breezes from, the western waters of the Manukau, these opened up to our sight

Maungakiekie

In fact, the name Maungakiekie (meaning mountain of the kiekie vine) has not been obliterated, and is in regular usage today. Maungakiekie was home to a very large and significant pā, although it was unoccupied due to tribal wars when Logan Campbell arrived at the Waitematā. The original tree on its summit, a sacred tōtara, was cut down by settlers for firewood, and replaced with a pine tree, which in turn was attacked by Māori protestors in the 1990s. It was removed in 2000. At its summit now stands an obelisk which marks the grave of John Logan Campbell.

A postcard showing Rangitoto in the distance, drawn in the 1880s.

Rangitoto, Auckland, New Zealand, 1904-1915, Auckland, by Muir & Moodie studio. Purchased 1998 with New Zealand Lottery Grants Board funds. Te Papa (PS.002366)

resembling a great inland lake hemmed in by the sea-coast range of high forest-clad land. Through a break in the range — the entrance, in fact, to the harbour, we got a glimpse of the sea on the west coast. Underneath us, away at the foot of the slope which stretched from where we stood to the shore, close to the beach we could see the blue smoke rising from the native settlement to which we were bound. We walked slowly down the winding, sloping footpath, endeavouring to understand the topography of the landscape which revealed the headlands of both the east and west coast, interlacing each other in a manner so puzzling that we were unable to unravel them and know which were which. The cool southerly wind blowing over the great Manukau basin we inhaled with positive physical enjoyment. In after-life I have only known such crisp delicious air when on alpine summits or Highland moorlands in early autumn with the first of the clear northerly

The first government settlement in Auckland, 1840.

E-216-f-115, Alexander Turnbull Library

winds. As we neared the settlement we walked through a large kumara plantation, and upon coming near the huts and being descried by the natives were welcomed with the customary cry of welcome, 'Haere mai, haere mai!' and waving of their mats. ...

We propounded the object of our visit — that we were not pig but land hunting, and furthermore that we had set out hearts on the Remuera slopes stretching down to Orakei [Ōrākei] Bay. But to the question, would they sell that land, a very prompt and decided 'Kahore' [kāhore] (No) was unhesitatingly given, but they would sell land farther up the harbour.

And for many a long year these Remuera slopes remained native-owned, and to this day part of Orakei Bay still is. And so we paddled back again, the chiefs accompanying us, for after having had such a long chase to find them we deemed it safe to bag our game there and then. We — the four 'cannies' [Scotsmen] — let Wepiha to do some trade 'korero' [kōrero, discussion] with the natives and follow after us along with the chiefs, whilst we at once started on our return — by the same path we had come that morning back to Orakei.

As we reached the base of Mount Remuera, which the footpath skirted, I proposed that we should venture a scramble to the summit; but of the other three cannies two were too cannie to face it, Cook and Makiniki [McInnes, another two Scottish land speculators] making straight for our camping ground, whilst we 'ither twa' [other two] braced the hill. It was pretty stiff scrambling over the top of high fern; for sometimes, when unable to creep through it, we had to trample over it as best we could, but at last we gained the crater-top.

Auckland Harbour, 1877.

New Zealand Graphic and Descriptive. Auckland Harbour., 1877, London, by Charles Decimus Barraud, C F Kell, Sampson Low Marston Searle & Rivington. Te Papa (1988-0004-7)

Ah! I shall never forget the feelings of gratified amazement with which I gazed on the wonderful panorama which lay revealed to my sight for the first time on that now long-ago day. 'Age cannot wither nor Time stale' its infinite beauty in my eyes. Since that day I have travelled far and wide, have stood on the Acropolis of Corinth and looked on its isthmus and sea on either shore. I have seen Napoli La Bella and didn't die, have gazed on panoramas from alpine and Appennine summits, but in later years, when I again stood on that selfsame spot on Remuera's Mount, and gazed across Waitemata's waters and its many islands to Rangitoto's Peaks and the Cape Colville Range, I confess that to me it surpassed all I had ever seen elsewhere — stood forth pre-eminent, unequalled, unsurpassed.

The sun now dipping behind the western coast ranges, and warming up in reddening glow Rangitoto's Peaks, warned us it was time to descend from our high estate in order to reach before it became dark the little tent which we saw as a white spot away down on Orakei beach. Regaining the footpath, we sped along down the slopes, and soon were enjoying a pannikin of tea which we found ready on our arrival at the camp.

Before very long Wepiha arrived, accompanied by the chiefs who on the morrow were to point out the land which they would be willing to sell. We did not allow the night to grow very old before the heaps of fresh fern upon which we had spread our blankets wooed us to luxurious rest.

I wot [know] those of us who did not sleep too soundly even to dream, dreamed of a fern wilderness suddenly converted into a smiling town, and down its handsome streets, by some strange confusion of ideas, we were all paddling in a canoe steered by Wepiha and the bottom of the canoe was well ballasted with bags of gold.

Tourist spots

The Acropolis of Corinth in Greece, the Bay of Naples (Napoli) and the Apennine Mountains in northern Italy were considered sites of extreme beauty in the nineteenth century. The expression 'see Naples and then die' was popular among wealthy travellers, who felt nothing could match its magnificence. Logan Campbell has a different opinion!

SOURCES AND FURTHER READING

Beaglehole, J.C., ed., *The Endeavour Journal of Joseph Banks 1768–1771*. Angus and Robertson, 1962.

Boultbee, John, *Journal of a Rambler, The Journal of John Boultbee*. Edited by June Starke, Oxford University Press, Auckland 1986, in association with the Alexander Turnbull Library Endowment Trust.

Campbell, John Logan, *Poenamo*. First published London 1881, republished Whitcombe and Tombs, 1952.

Cruise, Richard A., *Journal of a Ten Months' Residence in New Zealand*. Frst published London, 1824; Capper Press facsimile 1974.

Dieffenbach, Ernst, *Travels in New Zealand*. First published London, 1843; Capper Press facsimile 1974.

Drummond, James, John Rutherford: *The White Chief*. Whitcombe and Tombs, Christchurch, 1908.

Earle, Augustus, *Narrative of a Residence in New Zealand*. First published London, 1832; ed. E.H. McCormick, Oxford, 1966.

Maning, Frederick Edward, *Old New Zealand: A Tale of the Good Old Times*. Frst published Auckland, 1863; republished Whitcombe and Tombs, 1956.

Polack, Joel Samuel, *New Zealand: being a Narrative of Travels and Adventures*. In two volumes, first published London, 1838; Capper Press facsimile 1974.

Rawson, John Elder, ed., *The Letters and Journals of Samuel Marsden*. Dunedin, 1932.

Rogers, Lawrence M., ed., *The Early Journals of Henry Williams*. Pegasus Press, Christchurch, 1961.

Savage, John, *Some Account of New Zealand*. First published London 1807; Capper Press facsimile 1973.

Straubel, C.R., ed., *The Whaling Journal of Captain W. B. Rhodes*. Whitcombe and Tombs, Christchurch, 1954.

Wakefield, Edward Jerningham, *Adventure in New Zealand*. First published London, 1845; republished Whitcombe and Tombs, Christchurch, 1908.

PUBLISHER'S NOTE

Every care has been taken by the publisher to establish any residual ownership where the Copyright Act may still apply to the reprinting of any of this material. Any enquiries should be addressed to the publisher. The co-operation of the Alexander Turnbull Library with regard to the John Boultbee and Edward Markham material is gratefully acknowledged.

INDEX